MW01712842

I Love You Like a Brother

By Terry Flatt

ISBN: 979-8-558360-25-7

"I Love You Like a Brother is about the importance of relationships, respect and listening. It is about resilience, determination and advocacy. This a MUST read for those entering the community living field and others who want to understand the history of institutions and the community living movement."

Ellen Tarshis

Executive Director of Community Living, Victoria BC

I LOVE YOU LIKE A BROTHER

The Battle to Be Understood

By

Terry Flatt

For my Dad,

Robert (Bob) Donald Flatt

the greatest man I ever met.

With his unfailing compassion

and sense of humor,

he enriched the lives

of all who

knew him.

In my father's name, partial proceeds of this book will go to the Namaste Music Program

Contents

INTRODUCTION

"Never, never be afraid to do what's right, especially if the well-being of...a person is at stake. Society's punishments are small compared to the wounds we inflict on our soul when we look the other way"

Martin Luther King Jr

The following story is about an awakening. In most stories of this type, it's the hero who has the awakening, a realization. In this story it is the hero who, after 28 years of struggle, triggers this awareness in me. What I came to realize is that he was more than his behaviour. He was aggressive and hurt others on a large scale. His behaviour was communicating something was not right for him. Once this breakthrough of understanding happened the slow education of the system that held him down could begin. This education was not a simple matter. His aggression took center stage and when I attempted communicate to those making decisions that there was more to this person than his hostility, my voice was drowned out by his actions. He was asking for help and he received punishment, programing and pills for his request. What he was looking for was understanding, respect and love. In his 28 years being housed in institutions he got little of what he was looking for.

I write this story as the one who saw his needs not being met. I saw the motives behind his aggression, I saw and gave him what he was asking for. This was the easy part. The hard part was convincing those who had their minds made up regarding who this person was and how best to support him.

My intent with this book is to illustrate the challenges faced by a person with a developmental disability by shining a light on what hasn't worked in the past for him and others. I hope to illuminate a path for support systems to follow that focuses on the needs of persons with such challenges. The financial and human costs are high when we make mistakes, when we misjudge, misunderstand and fail to pay attention to and understand the needs of the individual. First we must find the person behind the behaviour. When this is done we have a better chance to figure out the most humane, compassionate and effective way to provide the supports needed.

It has been decades since institutions housing persons with developmental disabilities have been closed in my home province of British Columbia. However, there has been, talk of going back to bigger facilities supporting larger numbers of this community. This talk is almost always driven by financial considerations. The thoughts of being more cost-effective have in the past led to the erosion of their freedoms as well as their dignity. The hero of this story, after confounding experts on how to stop his aggressive ways, thought he would be best served in the same institution he went to when he was nine.

I have put in my opinions and – yes - judgements of others, not so much of them personally, but of their decisions and, at times, their motivations for these decisions. My hope in this effort is to educate those who do not know of the history of persons with developmental disabilities to inform them about the injustices of the past and how these offenses have left emotional and physical scars, on those deemed different.

In some cases I have changed the names of those involved. In other cases I have not. I have endeavored to protect the innocent as well as the guilty. In all cases the stories that follow are all true to the best of my recollection.

I felt I had a unique perspective on the journey of some folks who experienced this incarceration and what was called "support", but could better be described as systemic abuse. As a hands-on worker in an institution for the last 10 years of institutionalization (1982 to 1992), I was able to see the tail end of what it was like to live as a non-convicted prisoner. The other part of this effort is to describe my personal experiences with one particular person who had a rough time in these institutions as well as a turbulent transition from institutional to community living.

Institutionalization damaged him both physically and emotionally. Despite the discriminations and inequalities he had to endure he didn't stop fighting against it. He fought from 1969 till 1997. He may have lost most of the battles but he did win the war. He got what he wanted, or at least, he got what he needed. The abuse he faced was systemic. The system allowed what happened to him, they did not seem to see think what it was doing was cruel on the contrary, they viewed what they were doing to be helpful. His reply was to bide his time for personal payback to those who carried out what the system ordered or at least allowed to happen to him.

Too few seemed to want to try hard enough to get to the source, to understand why he behaved the way he did. I believe that he was sending a signal- like the trapped miner continuing to tap out an SOS with the hopes that someone will finally decipher the message. I heard and understood the message and I became his translator. My job was to convince others to hear and understand what I heard and comprehended. Some in positions of power refused to even listen to what I was communicating, what I was translating. I had the same problem as our hero, I had to fight to be heard.

This is a story of advocacy, of understanding and of love.

A BRIEF HISTORY

"Justice will not be served until those who are unaffected are as outraged as those who are."

Benjamin Franklin

Maya Angelou said "Don't hesitate to learn the most painful aspects of our history, understand it." With this in mind I will be giving just that, the distressing parts of history for persons with developmental disabilities and how they were seen and treated.

I will start off in Germany in the 1930s. The Nazis believed that eliminating persons with disabilities would strengthen society's ability to function more efficiently. They had propaganda that included posters, newsreels and cinema films showing persons with disabilities as "useless eaters" and having "lives unworthy of living." They stressed that there was something unhealthy and un-natural to have society pay to keep these people alive.

After this propaganda, action soon followed. Compulsory sterilization of persons with disabilities began in 1933. In 1934, the German and Austrian public health authority began to encourage parents of children with disabilities to admit them to specially designed and designated pediatric clinics. These clinics were just killing wards. With specially recruited medical staff, they would murder these young people by lethal overdoses or starvation. When the sterilization of adults and the killing of kids was not getting the economic results quick enough, the Nazis set up six death camps called "euthanasia centers." Persons with disabilities were the human guinea pigs that would lead the way for Hitler's "Final Solution." The intent was to rid society of those believed to be unwanted: Jews, Roma, homosexuals and the disabled. It is estimated that during this program 275,000 persons with disabilities were murdered by the Nazis. (1)

What the Nazis did was the extreme end of the spectrum, but in North America in the 1900s, the treatment of persons with developmental disabilities was also shameful and cruel. The eugenics movement in North America followed some of those theories, survival of the fittest. This was the justification for the forced sterilization, marriage restrictions and the warehousing of persons with developmental disabilities in institutions.

Like most systems there needs to be a way of measuring something in order to label it. Along came Alfred Binet, a French psychologist who around 1913, invented the IQ test.(2)This was used to identify students who required special help but was soon adapted to label persons with developmental disabilities. Dr. Henry H Goddard took this test to label 40 percent of the 1.75 million army recruits as "feeble-minded." Dr. Goddard was quoted as saying, "of late we have recognized a higher type of defective, the moron, and have discovered that he is a burden; that he is responsible to a large degree for many, if not all, our social problems." Goddard was quite a piece of work. He referred to persons with developmental disabilities as "the almosts," meaning that they were almost humans. (3)

Sub-humanization is a big word and the word itself tells you what it means. It comes in many different flavors. It has been used as a tool in war, sexual crimes, slavery, and psychological abuse. This then contributes to the misunderstanding of those deemed feeble-minded, and the labelling of ethnic or racial groups as being inferior. With this label of inferiority firmly in place the justification of institutionalization, sterilization, social segregation and abuse can flourish. The term, "de-humanization" came out in the early 19th century. When referring to a person or a certain group of people as non-human it is easy to deny that they have much or any distinctive human traits. Calling a person or a group of people animals or conceiving them as inanimate objects, paves the way for degradation and abuse. When we think of others as objects or animals, it then becomes acceptable to treat them in ways that we would not find permissible to treat our fellow humans. This takes away our inhibitions with regards to harming or exploiting them, hurting them and depriving them. We can easily treat them so because they don't have feelings like "us."

This type of language and action is meant to convince the public that these abuses are good policy. When Dr. Goddard published his educated sentiments as scientific fact, those with developmental disabilities did not stand a chance with regards to fair treatment by the systems they lived in, or by the public who believed what they read or were told.

During this time there were plenty of people like Dr. Goddard sounding the alarm that persons with developmental disabilities were less than human. Instead of extermination, which presumably would have caused an outcry from the public, they needed be housed in a less-than-human place. They needed to be locked away from the rest of the world. This was the birth of institutionalization for persons with developmental disabilities in North America.

The "inmates," as they were treated as such, had no rights. How could they have rights like other humans if they were deemed, by learned men, to be less than such? There was no need for dignity for these institutional prisoners and no need for privacy. It was often the thought that these folks could be fixed, cured or rehabilitated, so as these institutions got bigger they became more medicalized. The focus was to change these people rather than to accept them.

A CHANGE FOR THE BETTER

"Illegitimate freedom is only a different shade of bondage."

Kingsley Opuwari Manuel

What follows is a story of one who lived and one who worked in the institutions and their escape to a kinder, more understanding world. My intent is not to shock or shame, but to show, in all its ugliness, the sometimes horrible things we can do to other human beings and the ways these injustices were perpetrated in the name of medical practice or behaviour modification. These people who needed support always paid for this support with their freedom and dignity.

Knowing where we have been helps us to know where we are now. Having a grasp on the past and present can give us guidance on how to map the future. I am encouraged that there has been a strong grassroots of change driven by the self-advocate movement. Those with a developmental disability are no longer directed only by a hierarchical system made up of scholarly people in offices far away from those needing support. We now have a system of caregivers who are in direct contact with the people and are best able to understand and represent their needs. These caregivers, guided by their understanding, are now doing most of the directing.

The Oxford English Dictionary describes advocate as: 1. a person who publicly supports or recommends a particular cause or policy. 2. A person who pleads a case on someone else's behalf. It comes from the Latin word *advocare:* call (to one's aid). By the nature of the hierarchal system, those in faraway offices, could never be advocates as one cannot know the needs and wants of a person if they don't really know them as a person. The hierarchical system still exists but more and more it is the people themselves and those who know them best who are making evaluations about their lives.

One of our biggest mistakes was that, in the past, we believed we had to listen to and do the bidding of psychologists, doctors, or administrators. Even if we listened carefully to those we served, and understood their wants and needs better, we were mostly out of the decision-making process on how to best provide this support.

Thankfully, this has changed. Direct caregivers and their clients have a direct say in their care. Persons with developmental disabilities are now in a better places. The following story is of one man's journey from institutions to community and how he and those who knew him were, by design, kept out of the decision making process.

AN INSTITUTION BY ANY OTHER NAME

"The greater the power, the more dangerous the abuse."

Edmund Burke

With a peaceful sounding name like Woodlands School, one might conjure up a picture of a campus built within manicured forested grounds. Maybe the bustle of smiling students on their way to classes, dreaming of leaving this school one day with lessons learned that will guide their futures. The name, however, did not match the reality.

Woodlands School, as it came to be called, was built in 1878 as a provincial (British Columbia, Canada) lunatic asylum on 100 acres of government land. This patch was known as woodlands, hence the name. This was done at a cost of $24,000. The records show that those admitted to this building had the following disorders: nervous trouble, masturbation, injury to the head, intemperance (lacking self-control), fright and unknown. The building was a cold, grey English castle-like structure. It was castle-like from the outside at least. Inside? Not so much. It was designed to house loonies and masturbators, how fancy did it need to be?

In 1944 some extensive remodelling was started on the "school for Subnormals" and in 1950 this institution was renamed Woodlands School. During the 1950s a bunch of cottages were built. The names of such cottages were Pine, Beech and Willow in keeping with the Woodlands theme. They were called cottages but they were not small thatched roofed places, they were brick and concrete buildings with bars on the windows and skeleton keys to open the big metal doors. The windows were placed high to let in light but, unless on a ladder, one could not look out. These structures were to help with the overcrowding problem in the main building. In 1961, Woodlands School housed 1,436 people, which was to be its highest recorded population.

During the early 1960s Woodlands was nearly at full capacity. This was a huge group of very vulnerable people being looked after by a small group of mostly misguided caretakers. This caretaker group was misguided by the medical system and psychology professionals doing what they thought was the right thing to do. Using a hospital model for people who were not sick did not work well for those living there. (4)

The intention of Woodlands School, based on the choice of having "school" in the name, seems to be an attempt to treat the disability as a symptom that could be made to go away with the proper treatment or teachings. As a result, the treatments were designed for what people *were* not rather than for who they *were*.

I choose to believe that some who worked there did not have immoral intent. They were doing what was thought to be good and noble. I also understand it is easy, with hindsight, to see these efforts as wrong and I do not judge those who wrote up the plans for treatment, and I do not judge those charged with implementing these plans. I just see it for what it was: a mistake. A mistake based on the belief that those people were less than others. Plans were made to change the residents, to make them better. No one happily accepts being subjected to forced treatments or teaching methods that are only understood by those wanting to see change in the person. When these reluctant students failed to put up with these misguided efforts they were labelled "uncooperative" or "untrainable." Then, the help given, with good intentions, became a tool of oppression.

The following is an expert from Gregory, R. (2006, March 23) in an article in the Georgia Straight newspaper titled "Woodlands Justice in Doubt"

"Bill MacArthur was seven in 1963 when his mother left him for the first time at Woodlands School. His mother said it was a summer school but she didn't tell him he could not go home. Bill was hyperactive, but was also highly intelligent, and he soon learned the lessons of survival at Woodlands. "In the morning they would line us up for the washroom. I remember seeing people tied down to toilets and staff pouring hot water over their genitals to make them go. I was afraid all the time." "There was a nurse....she found a staff member in bed with a patient and she reported him. They fired her."

MacArthur said he was sexually assaulted by staff, but what he feared most was being forcibly submerged in tubs filled with ice water until he was nearly drowned, another boy he knew was repeatedly confined in a canvas sack and held under the water "this was the way they controlled your behaviour".

There was a report released in 2002 looking into the allegations of abuse at Woodlands called, "The Need to Know" (McCallum, D. (2002)

The Need to Know: Administrative review of Woodlands School. www.bcal.org/documents/woodlands_Abuse/The_Need_to_know)
The years of investigation were from 1975-1992, looking at the deaths and critical incidents, to try to locate if these events took place. The following are some excerpts of an article by Jake Adrian when speaking to Dulcie McCallum, the author of The Need to Know Report. She said "abuse had in fact occurred to the extent to be able to conclude that there was evidence of systemic abuse". She found in the records details of physical abuse such as "hitting, kicking, smacking, slapping, striking, restraining, isolation, grabbing by the hair or limbs, dragging, pushing, very cold showers and very hot baths resulting in burns to the skin, verbal abuse bullying, belittling, inappropriate conduct such as extended isolation, wearing shackles and a belt leash. There was documented evidence of injuries including bruises, scratches, broken limbs, black eyes and swollen face. The sexual abuse included assault, intercourse and, as a result, injuries and in a few cases pregnancy."

When asked why the abuse was not reported she found documentation of "a code of silence among the staff."

"There was an abuse policy in place and there was a so-called policy to investigate, but there didn't seem to be any attempt to actually proactively prevent abuse." She went on to say "although a parents group had come forward with policy around abuse, I could not find any evidence of safeguards, no reporting to police; no reporting to parents."

What she did find was, "quite a bit of documentation about discrediting the extent to which residents suffered harm compared to the way other, non-labeled people did. Staff assumed they (the residents) weren't smart enough to appreciate the trauma of being kicked, slapped or belittled."

As someone who knows people who lived in Woodlands before 1975, the dates this report studied, and based on what I was told by these survivors, it was as bad or worse in the 1950s and 60s. I interviewed a person who had volunteered at Woodlands in the early 70s and she said, "The cleaning of the residents was like an assembly line. Staff would undress the residents from their nighttime attire, then push them toward the person who had a soapy brush and a pail, and would mop them from head to toe, then they moved on to a staff who hosed them down, shoved them toward the staff doing the drying and then to the staff doing the dressing in their day clothes. This was not unlike a car washing facility." A sad way to start the day and for some it got sadder as the day went on.

Frank, whom I first met in 1982, was placed in Woodlands in 1953 at the age of five and any mention of Woodlands would illicit considerable agitation and negative talk from him. One of his comments to me was "How would you like to take it up the ass at five?" Frank told me of many abuses such as those in The Need to Know Report but the main thing he was pissed at was how horrible the food was. Frank would go on a rant and call what he was served at Woodlands as "slop." I took Frank's word regarding the grub. When Frank was on a vacation with me on a Gulf Island, he struck up a conversation with Tom, a man in his late 70s, the neighbour of the place we were staying. The conversation started with Tom, a curmudgeon, "What the hell are you doing wearing a tie?" he asked Frank, "I always do," Frank replied. You see, when Frank lived at Woodlands the supervisors wore white shirts and a black ties. That was their uniform. Frank would have seen the power these people had, and when he was able to choose his own clothes, that was what

Frank wanted. Frank had had enough of being told what to do and he wanted to dress the part of someone with power.

During their conversation, Frank mentioned to Tom that he used to live in Vancouver and eventually Woodlands came up. Frank went on his usual rant about the food and then went into the house to avoid any more talk about the place. Tom, a retired carpet-layer, went on to tell me why the food at Woodlands was so bad. He knew people who worked there and was told by them that after the food trucks came to deliver, some staff would help themselves to the good stuff and packed it to their cars. This would leave the cooks to make do with what was left, hence the slop Frank was so upset about.

Pat is another resident who lived at Woodlands the same time Frank did and he tells a story of how the staff would make his meals even worse by placing their cigarette butts in his slop. Pat was blind and could not only smell the butts but also hear the snickering of the staff who found this amusing. I asked Frank if, during special occasions like Christmas, they got better food and he replied "no, not even at Christmas." I guess the turkeys that were delivered ended up in the trunks of some staff's cars.

Behind the walls and fences the public knew little of what went on at Woodlands. Stories abounded regarding those who lived there. Some thought these folks were put there because they were dangerous to the public. They must be dangerous, or why would they be locked up? One such person was my older cousin Danny, a big guy who played football but was a gentle giant. In 1969 he was 17 and was working at his summer job at a gas station near Woodlands. His boss told him to go to the Woodlands staff parking lot to change a flat tire. He explained to me that he was scared to go. Scared to get close to a place that held these mostly unseen and, by all rumours, people that needed to be avoided. Danny tells me that it was the middle of summer and a beautiful day. He was relieved to find no danger lurking in the parking lot, and when he found the car in need of attention he soon had the car on the jack and set to work changing the tire. That was when, as Danny described, a tiny man came up to him and said, "Hi." Danny said "Hi" back and then proceeded to change that tire like he was on the pit crew in the Indianapolis 500. Danny tells how he was petrified. He then jumped into his truck, rolled the windows up on a hot day, and locked the doors. He says "I was told that these guys had superhuman strength." Danny told this story to me and felt very sheepish about it. “I just didn’t know.” Most didn’t know.

About 12 years later he knew better as he and his band would go behind the Woodland walls and entertain the residents. His sheepishness came from how wrong the rumours were and how he bought into them. His experience of playing music for the folks of Woodlands was the opposite of the stories he was told. Those living there did not need to be avoided they needed to be accepted. He was quick to learn that the superhuman strength they had was their ability to endure the imprisonment in addition to their disability and still be able to smile, laugh and dance.

HE GIVES AS GOOD AS HE GETS: BRENT'S STORY

"When someone disrespects you, beware the impulse to win their respect. For disrespect is not a validation of your worth but a signal of their character."

Brenden Burchard

This is where we meet Brent, the hero of the story. I am telling his story with his permission and the blessings of his family. I use his real name because he is real as is this story.

Wilfred Brent Smith was born on April 1, 1960, at Vancouver General Hospital in Vancouver. His delivery had complications. His mother had high blood pressure and was 40 years old which was old to have a baby in 1960. I was told, the doctor's first priority was to save his mother. Brent was perhaps held in the birth canal too long but after his delivery, he seemed fine. Two days later in the hospital, he suffered severe convulsions which most likely caused his brain damage. Soon after his birth he and his family moved to Victoria on Vancouver Island.

Brent did not develop at a normal level. He did not sit up for at least two years and he was in a walker for several years before he could walk. His speech was delayed as well. His mother worked with him

24 hours a day. He was a fulltime job for her and as he got older became physically strong; therefore he was hard to handle. There were medications available to help him calm down but they were very expensive and of course at that time there was no physical or financial help from the government.

He did attend Victor Street School for a few hours a day during the week, giving his mother a welcomed but small break. This respite, although helpful, was not enough for her to really get much rest. His physical behaviour was very difficult for his mom to control. This took its toll on her mentally and physically.

It was common for him to just turn over his chest of drawers into the room or slam his bedroom door 100 times in a row. His mom had to watch over him 100 percent of the time that he was awake. It was not an easy time for his family. There was no help for them from the government back in the 1960s. Brent was on numerous medications to try and help to improve his behaviours. His growing strength became more of an issue and his parents knew that they could no longer support him. The family struggled with the cost of Brent's medications and it took a toll on their financial well-being.

Brent had two siblings who were much older. Bruce was 17 and Sherry was 11 when Brent was born. Brent's sister remembers taking him for a walk one day in his wagon: "He climbed out and started hitting me and it was all I could do to get him back in and get him home."

Life was becoming a huge struggle for his parents who by now had serious financial problems with the escalating costs of Brent's medications. Also, they were older parents, in 1969 Brent's mom was 50 and his dad was 60. They did not have the stamina to support their son. Brent's brother and sister had left home by 1969 with families and careers to look after. Brent's mom and dad were on their own with regards to tending to Brent's needs.

Brent's sister said, *"Things had to change. The only place available at that time was an institution called 'Woodlands' in Vancouver, BC. It must have broken Mom and Dad's hearts the day that they took him over to Vancouver. It certainly was not a good experience for Brent. His aggressive behaviours were met with severe punishments. They repeatedly put him in a 'time out' room by himself. Mom and I visited him at Woodlands. He was so sad and unhappy! He didn't understand why he couldn't come home with us! It was heartbreaking."*

Brent was 9 years old in 1969 when he was placed in Woodlands. It was suggested to the family that they not visit Brent for at least three months to allow him to settle in his new place. Brent's sister tells of the first visit three months after Brent's arrival at Woodlands. *"I could hardly recognize him. His face was beat up and swollen pretty bad."* When Brent's family questioned how this happened, they were told by the person in charge of his ward that, *"he gives as good as he gets."* Brent spent the next three years at Woodlands getting as good as he gave.

Due to overcrowding at Woodlands, another facility was built in Brent's hometown of Victoria and in 1972 he was transferred there. This sparkling new institution was called Glendale Lodge. This institution was state of-the art as institutions go. Even though the process of deinstitutionalization (shutting them down and moving those residents to the community) was in the works in 1972 the need for dealing with overcrowding had to be addressed, hence Glendale Lodge.

It was the disability rights movement that challenged the provincial government to close institutions. This need for social change was powered by the human rights revolution, the strong parents groups and self-advocates, as well as the studies showing institutionalization had negative impacts on those who lived there and to those who worked there. There was plenty of interest by government and advocates to shut these places down, the challenge was how to do it. It was a very complex process that required the involvement of many stakeholders.

THE BIRTH OF GLENDALE LODGE

"The secret to change is to focus all your energy not on fighting the old, but on building the new."

Socrates

What's in a name? Woodlands School had no graduates. Glendale Lodge had no large stone fireplaces or fancy leather couches. There were no trophy salmon hanging on the walls as one might find in a luxury fishing lodge. There may have been nice furniture in the offices of the high-priced help but where the residents lived, not so much. As in the case of Woodlands School, the addition of the word Lodge it would seem that they wanted to take the edge off of what this building was. My dad said, "You can dip a dog turd in chocolate but that don't make it dessert."

What Glendale wasn't, was Woodlands. Oh, it had similarities: it was a big building that housed persons with developmental disabilities but the main difference was the staff culture. As mentioned in the Need to Know Report, the code of silence among staff, the abuses that would not be reported, and the indignities that were inflicted without reprisal were not the same at Glendale.

You see, this was 1971, and the facility was the first of its kind in Victoria. This place needed to be staffed, so a call went out to those wishing to work there. I interviewed some Glendale staff that applied for employment because of that advertisement. They told me that after a successful interview they had to take a three-month course or training session on what their job would be and how they were expected to do this job. I was told that the majority of the hands-on staff were "young, in their 20s, keen and idealistic, kind of hippy-like." The 60s were a time of changing attitudes regarding human rights. These young staff lived through these times and needed little convincing that those they were going to be supporting deserved the same respect and dignity that all citizens had.

The new residents mostly came from Woodlands and they came in groups where they were assessed, then placed in what were called "lodges." This was the name given to the wards, the sleeping, eating and hanging-out areas. People were placed in lodges that were designed to efficiently meet the health care and safety needs of the individual. Those not able to walk and who needed help with all areas of care, feeding, personal care and such, would be put in lodges that would specialize in this type of attention. Those who could walk and look after their own toileting and could feed themselves were separated into categories or levels of competency: Could they talk; did they have behaviour issues such as biting, hitting or other types of aggression towards others. There were 13 lodges at Glendale so there was a place that would be able to accommodate all. Folks would move around if it was found a particular lodge was not the right fit.

I asked these former staff who were among the first at Glendale if they saw any actions or policy that would not be accepted today and the answer was "Other than some behaviour modification techniques, no." They said "some staff were less compassionate than others," but they saw no blatant abuse. These two 1971 staff also worked at Woodlands but this was after they had worked a few years at Glendale. They both moved to Vancouver to further their education and they got part-time work at Woodlands. I asked about the difference between the two institutions. One woman said Glendale was a place where staff were encouraged to personally interact with the residents, there were parties where staff would play live music, and they would have lodge barbecues and such. She went on to say this was not her experience at Woodlands. She told of a time she was on a ward at Woodlands and had a young girl sitting on her lap and she was brushing her hair. This staff was in her early 20s at the time. While she was tending to this young girl, a long-time Woodlands staff came up to her and forcibly yanked this girl off her lap, grabbed the hair brush and wacked the young girl on the head and said, "this is how we brush their hair here." This young staff was shocked then she was told, "We don't do this,"- this meaning being nice-"cause they will expect it from us all the time." One of the other things she saw that was different was that although Glendale had "time-out" rooms, she witnessed residents spending days in these rooms at Woodlands, with only a straw mat to lie on. This echoes the information in the Need to Know Report.

The other ex-Glendale staff I interviewed said he did not witness that type of culture when he worked at Woodlands in the late 70s as he was on the extended care wards. These wards were run by nurses and they provided good care, as they were trained to do. It would appear that the majority of abuse inflicted on those living at Woodlands would be the folks that could walk or talk. I would suggest that the training most Woodlands staff received was from their fellow long-time workers.

This shows that better planning and guidance, as well as a change in attitude, can make a huge difference. The culture of Glendale was new and those working there were young. The culture of Woodlands was old and, as the Need to Know Report stated, you don't rock the boat in a place that is set in its ways. Glendale was a new, clean sheet of ice with fresh-faced players with ideas and ideals that had left the 50s and 60s behind.

IF WE KNOW BETTER WE DO BETTER

"A reform is a correction of abuses; a revolution is a transfer of power."

Lofton Bulwer

In 1972, Brent arrived to his new digs and by all accounts he came in swinging. The lyrics of a Pink Floyd song "All that you touch and all that you see… is all that your life will ever be." In Brent's three years in Woodlands he was touched in aggressive and damaging ways. All that he saw was abuse, toward him and others. In his mind why would Glendale be any different than where he just came from?

Those I spoke to remember a not-so-big but strong, skinny kid. He was smart inasmuch as he would not telegraph his strikes, be it a head-butt or a punch. Brent needed his targets to be close and any long run would alert intervention or escape by the intended target. It was in Brent's notes that, "he would stalk his victims." Knowing Brent as I do now, I would suggest that he had a reason for his aggression towards others. It may not have been a good one but he had one, I am sure. I am also sure that if a staff or a fellow resident did him a dirty, Brent would, in Gordie Howe-type fashion, bide his time to get his retribution. Howe once said "I don't get even, I get back." Howe's son tells a story of how he witnessed his dad during the opening faceoff wack his direct opponent without provocation. His son asked him, "Why. The game had not started. He did nothing to you." "Well, for one reason the referee had his back to me and also I wanted to get him before he got me." I believe that was Brent's thinking as well. Get them before they get me.

Brent spent plenty of hours in the time out room. Every lodge had its own time-out room but on a "behavioural" lodge where residents could display challenging behaviour it was well used. The idea of time-out was to have a place where a person would settle or calm down, to take them away from the environment that perhaps caused whatever indiscretion they were guilty of. The time-out rooms at Glendale were approximately 8 ft. by 8 ft., a hard floor, a frosted small window to the outside and a small window in the door. This window on the door had a curtain on the outside so staff could look in when they wanted but the person inside the room had no ability to look out. The use of time-out was presented as helping those who are out of control. This depends on what your idea of helping is. If this was a teaching tool the main thing it taught the residents was that might makes right.

Staff are told they needed to remove the client in a neutral way, using neutral tones and words. The person was to be handled like an object that needed to be put in the closet. This act of isolation was presented as a positive intervention for the person being isolated and the time limits to this isolation were handed down from people who have the qualifications to make such decisions. Five, 10 or 30 minutes, giving the person the right amount of time to calm down. If the end game was to help the person get away from some stress that caused the incident, a less formal way of stress release, e.g., a walk, a distraction perhaps could have been explored. Sadly, this rarely happened.

After a while, Brent would be able to spend more time in the general population of his lodge. Brent lived with 24 other men who could walk. Some, like Brent, could talk. And almost all had some kind of behavioural issues. I speculate that when Brent was at Woodlands he was not taken safely to the time-out room in a neutral way. I speculate that those staff at Woodlands would have used more force than was needed and gave Brent a few licks before locking the door. From what I know of Brent he would remember this and get back at this staff when the time was right. Brent would have a target upon his release. Brent did stalk staff at Glendale but he also had issues with some of his roommates, and the lessons of violence learned in Woodlands served him well when he deemed it necessary.

Glendale, and its different and gentler culture, gave Brent less time in isolation and more time with his peers. In the words of Maya Angelou "Do the best you can until you know better. When you know better do better." In the case of the move from Woodlands to Glendale, the staff knew better so they did better when it came to the responsibility of supporting those in their care.

MY PAVED ROAD TO GLENDALE

"Always go with the choice that scares you most, because that is the one that is going to help you grow."

Caroline Myss

Brent's road to Glendale was gravel and full of potholes, mine was by choice and very nicely paved.

In 1981 I was working in a lumber mill about an hour's drive from Glendale. At that time my job was working as a boom man (there were no boom women in those years). With the help of a pike pole, a long aluminum pole with a sharpened end and sharpened hook, I pushed and pulled logs in the water and fed them into the mill.

I enjoyed the job. I was outside and away from the noise of the saws. It was physical work and I liked that. The mill was built in 1914 and was refurbished in the mid-1930s. It was designed to accept the larger old-growth trees. I was smart enough to know this employment was on its last legs. The big logs were running out. This was 1980 and I knew I needed to find another line of work.

On the side I was dabbling in becoming a professional hockey referee, a long shot for sure. I did officiate at a high level and even did two pre-season NHL games. I think my officiating experience helped with understanding how to calm heated situations with the right words and tones at the right times. I would learn the names of the players who were the most aggressive or the ones who were the most volatile. I had a situation where I was attempting to break up a fight-one was receiving punches, one was giving them. I learned the giver's nickname was "Cow." He was very strong and I was no match for his strength. My ability to stop him physically was not going to work so

I said "Hey Cow, don't you think he's had enough?" By using his name I made contact with him and he stopped his aggression.

I also learned to be honest to calm the testosterone-fueled men when they disagreed with me. I recollect a game where I made a bad call but you can't put the toot back in the whistle. As the player was coming to me with his grievance I told him, "Hey you are right, it was a terrible call, Tracy." This seemed to stop him in his tracks. I used his name, I told him that he had a right to be upset. With Tracy now in the penalty box, the captain came to give me an earful regarding my poor decision, at which point Tracy stood up and said, "Hey, It's okay, he said he was wrong." Honesty works as a way to connect positively with the players. Another situation where being honest helped was when I was scheduled to referee a competitive men's league game. I had the flu and could not get a replacement official. With this illness my head was foggy and my ability to predict and react to a foul being committed was compromised. I was missing penalties. The captain during a stoppage of play came up to me and before he could speak I said "I know what you are going to say, I am horseshit tonight" I went on to tell him that I am doing my best but had the flu. So the game continues and again I miss a call right in front of the team's bench that had the captain talk to me. The foul I missed was against one of their players. The bench all stood up to yell their complaints and the captain said to them "sit down boys, he's not feeling good".

I learned that when things were getting heated I needed to have tools to cool things down. Using a player's name and being honest worked wonders. I listened to their concerns and didn't brush aside their complaints. Also when a player or coach would say, "Hey ref" I would not call them coach, I would use the coach's name. I would ask them to call me by my name so as to make a human connection. I was not "ref", I was Terry, a person like them.

In the heat of a competitive game when a person is upset, honesty is needed not bullshit. I had no idea that having these skills would be the base of how I would have success in my next line of work.

I also worked in some hockey schools teaching kids to skate. A parent of a child who had a developmental disability asked me to teach his son to skate. I said I would and we would go to the public skating sessions together. Although Dale did not learn to be a good skater, I had never had a student try so hard. We had a blast, lots of laughs. He was frustrated at first with falling down so much. I told him that the more you fall the more you learn. After one session he said to me, "I must have learned a lot today."

I was telling this story to a friend who lived in Victoria and he told me about Glendale. I had no idea it existed. Kent worked for a company that mowed the lawns there. He explained that they were always looking for support staff and males in particular. He passed on the number of the director of nursing to me and I called. Robert said we should meet and a date and time was set.

I was met by Robert at the front doors of Glendale and he took me on a tour. This was an experience for me. I had never seen folks like this. I was not shocked or scared, I was intrigued.

After the tour Robert said that I could apply right then and would likely get hired with no experience, so long as I had passed a criminal record check. He explained that if I did then I would be trained on the job. I was not sure of jumping right in like that. He mentioned that I could also take a 10-month course at the local college. He explained that someone forgot to delete the previous year's students from the computer so when anyone applied, they were told it was full. When classes began at the beginning of September there were only a handful of students. They were in need of filling the seats.

Robert gave me directions to the college and the name of the woman I was to meet. I met Lilly, a tiny woman who was one of the two main instructors of the course. She seemed to size me up quickly and must have thought...he's not much but he has a pulse, he'll do. Before I knew it she had talked me into registering, albeit two weeks after the course had begun. I left Victoria, went to the mill, quit, and then started classes the next day.

I was 24, and six years out of high school. I was never a good student as I have a mild form of dyslexia and was poorly prepared for post-secondary education. The first semester was more academic in nature, brain stuff, psychology and an English course. I did not get how it worked. I could not understand that even though I had to pay to sit in class for six to eight hours a day, I also had to do homework. I was lucky to have support from some of my classmates and they helped me limp through. I passed all courses but one, the one on the brain. I went on to the next semester and these classes were less academic and more practical, so I did better. The third semester was practicum, hands on support, free labour. Our choices were a placement in the community or at Glendale. I chose Glendale and loved it. My book learning was not so good but when it came to my interaction with the residents at Glendale, now that is where I shined.

I was nearing the end of the third and last semester and dreading having to go back to the college to take the class that I failed, I needed a passing grade to get my certificate. During my last practicum I was asked to come to the college and attend a meeting with the Dean of Community Services. Both my instructors were there. Turns out I got rave reviews from my practicum supervisors at Glendale and with this the instructors were able to convince the Dean to up my grades the little bit that was needed for me to obtain a pass of that class. Yes, insert fist pump…certificate earned.

I had great instructors at college. They realized that I was as green as a pool table, as were most of the students when it came to knowledge of persons with developmental disabilities. We were taught things such as: persons with Down syndrome had an extra chromosome and epilepsy was an interruption of the way the brain normally functions, and such. The thing that was most important to learn was, people are people no matter their abilities or lack of abilities.

In the early days of this course, our class took a tour of Glendale and we spent some time on an extended care lodge. These folks were unable to do much for themselves. Staff did the feeding, cleaning and making the residents comfortable.

We had a wide range of ages in our class: some right out of high school, others (like myself) in their mid-20s and some students in their 40s and 50s. While on this lodge an older student, perhaps in her 50s with what appeared to be a strong eastern European accent said out loud, "Why do they keep these people alive?" I am sure our instructor heard this as this student was not in the class the next day. This student did not have the understanding that a person is a person regardless of abilities.

I could not say that at that time I completely understood this myself until I met Lisa. We were learning about augmentative communication, sign language and a thing called Bliss. Bliss was a board that had words or pictures that a person could point to or indicate towards in order to communicate the words or actions they wished to get across.

When Lisa was born the doctors told her parents to put her in an institution and carry on with their lives. She had severe cerebral palsy and the only thing she could control was her eyes. The doctors said she was probably brain dead or close to it. Lisa's parents saw something the trained health professionals did not see. They kept her at home and discovered that she had control of her eyes. With this realization they had conversations with her and like any child the language part of her fully functional brain understood what was being said to her. With her fully functional eyes, ears and brain Lisa was able to respond in her limited way.

Our class met Lisa on a Friday afternoon. I did understand the concept that a person is a person regardless of abilities but all I really saw when I looked at Lisa was a woman in a body that betrayed her. Her limbs were pulled into strange positions, her hands and feet contorted. Our instructor asked us to converse with her. Her communication board consisted of about 300 words. There were four blocks of colors; red, blue, yellow and green. On the left of the board were numbers and on the top there were letters. In order for Lisa to give you the word she wanted to communicate, you would start off asking, "is it in the," then go through the colors. When you got to the block where the word was she would move her eyes up to the right which meant "yes". So when you narrowed it down then you listed off the numbers till she indicated "yes," then the letters. This would get you to the word she wanted to convey.

I asked the first question, "What are you doing this weekend?" So after going through the process of colors, numbers and letters Lisa came up with this answer: "tomorrow, outing, too #@*& early." Now these symbols meant a swear word and seeing as I had just left a logging town, my swear word of choice was, to fit her sentence, "fucking." As in, it was "too fucking early" for her to get up on Saturday!

It was this word that helped me to fully understand that Lisa and I are the same. Before that I only saw how we were different. I guess she could have meant it was too darn early or too bloody early. However, from where I came from my choice fit nicely. I know people who without that word, or a variation of that word, could not form a sentence.

Lisa was a part of Glendale but only in the form of a day-care situation, allowing her parents a break from the care she needed. But

Glendale was never her home. When at Glendale, Lisa would watch the soap operas with the staff and with her communication board she would describe a character as a bitch or an asshole. Lisa found joy in her life, she knew what she wasn't and she knew what she was, a person who deserved the same understanding, respect and dignity as anyone else.

My time at college taught me plenty but it was Lisa who taught me that when supporting others, to really look behind the eyes, away from the disability and to see the person. When I had the opportunity to work on these extended care lodges I would consider all living there to have the same fully functioning brain as Lisa. I would, while doing my tasks with these folks, be gabbing away to them about how badly the Canucks played the night before or whatever was the topic of the day. I would use their names, ask them questions knowing I would not get any answers. On a few occasions I was told by other staff, "they don't understand anything you are saying." My reply was, "And how do you know that?" It was my belief and hope that when those lying in their beds would see me they would think, "I hope he comes to my bed. I like it that he talks to me as though I understand because I do." They also could have thought "I hope he does not come over here, he never shuts up!"

If the person's brain was fully functioning but he or she lacked control over their limbs or facial expressions and had no ability to vocalize like Lisa, but still had ears and eyes and touch, which worked just fine. They would benefit, like we all do, with soft tones in our conversation, smiling faces accompanied by gentle touch.

To be in a body that is not well connected to the ability to communicate outwardly, then to have someone make the attempt to connect, must be a treat. I may not have been giving anyone a treat but how would I know. My hope was that in making the attempt that was a treat. I am sure there were many at Glendale who, like Lisa, just observed the world in the position of this one-way communication.

When I first met Lisa I knew very little about Buddhism but after traveling in Nepal I became more aware of this way of looking at life. The Art of Happiness, a book by Howard C. Cutler, quotes the Dalai Lama on the topic of establishing empathy for others, *"Whenever I meet people I always approach them from the standpoint of the most basic things we have in common. We each have a physical structure, a mind, emotions. We are all born the same way, and we all die. All of us want happiness and do not want to suffer. Looking at others from this standpoint rather than emphasizing secondary differences such as the fact that I am Tibetan, or different color, religion, or cultural background, allows me to have a feeling that I am meeting someone just like me. I find that relating to others on that level makes it much easier to exchange and communicate with one another."*

My dad was no Dali Lama yet he had the same idea of relating to others. The way my dad liked to exchange or communicate with others was to see if he could be of any help. I remember being about 5 years old on a cold, rainy, winter evening driving along a busy highway in Vancouver. There was a car on the side of the road with a flat tire. My dad would have been in his late 20s at the time and he was working as an iron worker. He was young and strong and he knew his way around wrenches. He pulled over to help. There were four of us kids in the back seat. I remember my mom questioning him about stopping. His reply was, "helping out." He left the car to do just that. I vividly recollect looking out the window in the rain and the drops on the window distorting the lights of the cars zooming by. I recollect my mom's displeasure of my dad's decision. This was a dangerous situation as the room to pull over was small and the chance for misfortune was great. When my dad got back in the car, soaked to the bones he was smiling. He got an earful from my mom: why did he help; he didn't know those people. I don't remember the exact words but it was along the lines of: you don't help because you know them; you help because they could use it. He was never happier than when he was helping others. He loved to pay things forward before it was a catchy phrase to say.

My mom, although she thought that helping out these strangers with tire trouble was dangerous, she had her moments of helping strangers. She, for a few years, was the go to person for youth who were in need of emergency temporary housing. A social worker would show up at our house with a young person, anywhere from 10 to 16 years old and for whatever reason they could not live with their parents. Their stay would last for a week or a few months until a more permanent place could be found. They were feed well and they had to follow certain rules. Jim arrived and he was really old to me, he was 15 and I was about five. Jim had to leave his parents' home as his dad was physically abusive to him and he had bounced around from house to house for a few years before he came to us. Jim had also gotten in trouble with the law, shoplifting cigarettes. This was the mid-1960s and the negative effects of this weed had yet to be announced publicly. My mom knew Jim smoked and she knew about his law breaking in order to obtain them. She also knew that Jim was kicked out of other homes because he found the rules in these homes too controlling. My mom made the rules of our house easy for Jim to follow. He had to clean up after himself, be nice to her kids and show her respect. She also told him that as long as he does those things she would also buy him his cigarettes. If he had them he would not steal to get them.

Jim was a greaser, slick backed hair and kind of long for the times, he wore a leather jacket tight jeans white t-shirt and pointy black shoes. He came in defiant but soon realized that the food was good and the rules of the house he could live with.

Jim stayed with us for about 4 months and when he turned 16 he was allowed to quit school and get a job. He was hired full-time at a tire shop and after a few pay cheques he moved out and got his own place.

About ten years would go by when there was a knock at the door and there was Jim with his wife and two kids. He had taken the effort to seek out our family as we had moved from the old house. He wanted to come and thank my mom for what she had done for him. He was an angry person when he came, he felt that all his life he had been neglected and no one cared much about him. Jim like Brent had only been treated with violence and he rebelled. Punishment followed the rebellion. He told my mom that she was the first adult in his life that really listened to him and treated him with respect. It was those two things that changed the direction he was headed. This would also be the things that Brent needed as well.

HELLO DARKNESS MY OLD FRIEND

"Nothing can dim the light that shines from within."

Maya Angelou

I first met Brent in 1982. I was 24, fresh out of college and loaded with the newest information regarding supporting persons with developmental disabilities. I must say we as a society were not that progressive that year, seeing as the 10-month course I took was called the MNRT program, which was short for Mental Retardation Worker.

Upon graduation I applied to work at Glendale. As a young male I was placed on a male behavioural lodge. Brent was not on this lodge but it was a sister lodge to Brent's, so staff were interchangeable. One afternoon I was summoned to Lodge Six, Brent's lodge. I arrived and it took Brent little time to notice a new face and he came right up to me and said, "Hello darkness," then grabbed my hand and led me to the locked cabinet where the record player was. I was unclear what Brent wanted. A regular staff saw what was happening and came to translate. She told me that Brent wanted to listen to Simon and Garfunkel and "Hello darkness" was the first line in one of their songs. I thought this to be a reasonable request. It was after I opened the cabinet and was searching for the record that a more senior staff came and rather rudely closed the door and locked it. He then explained to me that Brent couldn't listen to music, he had been bad. It seemed odd to me that this would be used as a behaviour modification tool. As mentioned before, Glendale was not Woodlands but it was an institution and as such the control of those living there was one of the main objectives. Taking away things that they liked was a form of obtaining control.

REMOVE HIS BALLS

"One's dignity may be assaulted, vandalized and cruelly mocked, but it can never be taken away unless it is surrendered."

Michael J. Fox

I spent most of my time on Lodge Two. Some 25 men occupied this space and they were to be kept under control. Certain boundaries were written in their behaviour-modification "programs" and if any resident stepped outside those boundaries there was protocol to follow and consequences for this transgression. In our lives, outside the institution, we have boundaries we must stay in and if we step out of line we go to jail, our freedom is taken away. When you live in an institution your freedom is already taken away so some other form of consequence is needed. This seemed to be the focus of the behaviour changers; to find something else to be taken from those living there.

This is how it seemed to work in my early days at Glendale; find out what they liked, then use this knowledge as a bargaining chip for better behaviour. When a resident stepped out of line or crossed the boundary noted in their behaviour modification programs, it set in motion the systemic thievery to happen.

The following is an example of one such program. David was 30 when I met him. He was born deaf and had a developmental disability. It was determined at the age of two that Woodlands was the best place for him. He spent 15 years there, like Brent, he was transferred to Glendale. David was a stocky fellow and, like most living in institutions, was not given much credit for being intelligent. He was unique inasmuch as he had possessions-things that were his-or at least he felt them to be his. Being new to the lodge I was to read all the behaviour programs for the guys. I laughed as I read David's program. It said the following: "When David misbehaves (no real details on what misbehave meant) his balls are to be removed." I quickly found out that the balls in question were not the ones attached to him but two balls that he appeared to adore, his possessions. One ball was an orange road hockey ball. The other was a soft rubber ball, blue with a red-and-white stripe. He would always have them in his hands except when eating. During mealtimes he would place them strategically so they were always in his sight while at the table. When going to bed they would be placed under his pillow.

David would sometimes violate, in some way, the misbehaviour guidelines and this would have him placed in the time-out room. I witnessed one such time where the old-school charge nurse was escorting him to the tiny room, in a less-than-gentle way. David had his prized possessions in his hands and before his lockup, as per behaviour protocol, his balls were removed. Upon completion of his time in solitary, the door was opened and, as per the program, his possessions were returned to him by the person who took them away. What I saw next was a bit shocking and profound. I saw David look at the balls, now in his hands, then glared at the nurse. David not taking his eyes off the nurse, tossed the balls on the floor and walked away. Now, I cannot say what David was thinking but I suspect it went something like this. "You asshole. I'm locked up here, with nothing that I care about but these two balls that, I cherish and you, at a whim, take them away from me. Well, fuck you. I am not going to give you the satisfaction of doing that again." These balls were offered up to David after but he refused to touch them after that incident.

OFF THE LIST

"It's hard to imagine a more stupid or more dangerous way of making decisions than by putting those decisions in the hands of people who pay no price for being wrong."

Thomas Sowell

There was also the "Van Ride," a treat that was used as reward and punishment- the punishment being that it would be taken away for an indiscretion. Brent still uses these punishment words: "You're off the list." He will say it when he is pissed off at himself or a staff. Staff at Glendale would sometimes let a resident know that they were on the list for the rare weekly ride away from the institution however, if their behaviour was not up to the standards then, "Off the list."

This van ride, or outing, happened once a week, after dinner. Lodge Two's day was Wednesdays. Two staff would load up the six people who made the cut in the big blue van with huge letters telling the public that this was a GLENDALE van.

This was a two-hour trip and staff were given spending money to purchase a treat. In my early years we had strict orders to not let them out of the van. Since the public was able to see the advertisement of where this van was from they were also able to see the folks inside with their noses pressed against the windows looking at a world that they were not allowed to be in. In later years we were able to let the resident's out. I likened these outings in this way the vans were blue pods that would leave the mother ship Glendale, so those residing in this ship could get a small glimpse of the world they were kept away from.

THE BATTLE OF FORK AND SPOON

"An unhealed person can find offense in pretty much anything someone does. A healed person understands that the action of others has absolutely nothing to do with them. Each day you get to decide which one you will be."

Unknown

I have another story regarding David. He was described in his profile as being stubborn. Now I have come to discover that in the world of institutions, stubborn just means the person can be non-compliant, refuse to do as they are told, or wants to do things their way. In the world outside those walls these traits would have been described as this person was determined, strong willed or independent.

On Lodge Two there was a staff who had been working at Glendale from the beginning in 1972. He was a bossy fellow and controlling not only towards the residents but to the other less-senior staff. He was the "group leader" of David's group. This meant he was in charge of David's meal time. This staff had strict rules regarding the dining table etiquette.

This story takes place over the breakfast meal. All residents are seated, then the first course is offered. But first the resident has to say, or in David's case sign "please." A bowl of powdered scrambled eggs was placed in front of David and this is where things went sideways for him. David picked up the big spoon that was placed on the table, and proceeded to dig in. The "group leader" snatched the spoon from his hand and replaced it with the fork that was also on the table. You see, this staff had decided that David and all others at his table were to use the fork for this part of his breakfast. The spoon was for the porridge which was the next course. David, having thought this through, knew that the eggs were hard to stab with the fork and this utensil was ill-equipped to successfully bring the eggs to his mouth without most or some of the eggs falling off the fork. Having the eggs fall off was one problem. The other was if they fell off and landed on the table: these table eggs were to be left alone because if one ate anything off the table that was cause for immediate banishment by this group leader. David, not wanting spillage, put the fork down and picked up the spoon again. This was met with the staff, displaying annoyance, again taking the spoon from David and replacing it with the fork. Now, David was smart enough to know what this staff was trying to teach him but the staff had no clue what David was trying to teach this staff. David, being experienced with these eggs, found the spoon to be a better tool for the job. The staff had other ideas. Don't get me wrong, table manners have a place in society. The way some would dine in years past would be a reflection on their upbringing or station in life. In the 1800s, at a formal dinner, if a person was seen using the wrong utensil for the course in front of them, others would notice and he or she would be outed as having poor breeding and not be invited back. To the best of my knowledge David was not being taught this table etiquette for some future dinner date with royalty. David, after the third time being unable to teach the staff, was removed from the table for insubordination and had to wait until lunch to eat. Other staff, of course, would set aside food for David and he would get it when this controlling staff would go for his break.

When traveling through Asia I would send post cards to the lodge. I directed this card to David and it was a shot at this controlling staff, it read; "I am in Malaysia and you would love meal time here, you would not get kicked away from the table for eating with your hands as that is the way they eat in the small villages in this country". I hope it had the desired affect but I would guess that this staff was too daft to get this slight.

THE SHEET OF HIS DREAMS

"Of the seven deadly sins, lust is the pick of the litter."

Tom Robbins

A year went by before I encountered Brent again. I was on the night shift from 11 p.m. to 7 a.m. I was seconded to his lodge that night and after talking to the staff leaving and getting the rundown on my duties I did the mandatory walk around the sleeping men. I must have disturbed Brent because he got up soon after and I suspect again that he saw a new face and would try to get something over on me. I was right. He came up to me and there was no idle chit chat, Brent went right into what he wanted. "Get him a white sheet." I saw no reason to not grant him this request. Off I went to the linen room to look for a white sheet. Oddly enough there were no white sheets. I brought Brent a light yellow sheet thinking that would be good enough. He said "No, a white one." It seemed that Brent was determined to get a sheet in the colour of his preference and I felt that was the only way he would stop bugging me was to get him one. I called another lodge and asked if they had any in his desired colour. The woman on the other lodge said yes and that she would deliver it. Brent and I both waited by the door. She arrived, handed over the sheet. Brent took the sheet from me and without as much as a thank you he left with a smile on his face and a twinkle in his eye and off to bed he went.

Later that evening the woman who delivered the sheet gave me some valuable information. I was told why I could not find a sheet of that colour on Brent's lodge. Turns out that because of Brent no white sheets were delivered there. Brent would, with the help of a crisp white sheet, masturbate. It was this type of sheet that would float his boat. After hearing this I was a bit disappointed in Brent's manners. I had set him up with the sheet of his dreams and not a thank you came my way.

Institutions had a thing about masturbation. It was discouraged; hence, no white sheet for Brent. Now a little history about masturbation and persons with developmental disabilities. In the 19th century, Dr. Harvey Kellogg-yes the inventor of the Cornflakes that bear his last name-was uncomfortable with sex believing it was, "Unhealthy for the body and mind." He thought sex was bad and masturbation was way worse. He wrote, "Self-pollution is a crime doubly abominable." The good doctor worked at Battle Creek Sanitarium in Michigan. I guess those locked up there were open masturbators (I suppose they had little ability to find privacy). Dr. Kellogg went looking for a cure for this detestable crime. He believed that a healthy lifestyle could cure most ailments. He thought that meat and richly flavored food increased sex, and desire while plainer foods could help purify a person away from pleasuring himself or herself. Apart from the diet he had other ideas. For girls he recommended applying carbolic acid to the clitoris to burn it. For the boys he suggested threading silver wire through the foreskin to prevent erections. Cornflakes were made and fed to those in the sanitarium he worked at. This was done with the hopes of curbing the inmates touching themselves. In my research I found no statistics on how well the Cornflakes diet did in lowering the masturbation rates but I must confess I ate plenty of cornflakes in my youth and it did not slow down my interest in myself! (5)

THAT'S THE WAY WE HAVE ALWAYS DONE IT

"Pride is concerned with who is right. Humility is concerned with what is right."

Ezra Benson

I digressed a bit and the Kellogg story was long ago but some things done at Glendale were not too modern either. When I started at Glendale I was confused at a contraption Peter had to wear to bed. Peter was a big gentle guy and during the day he wore normal attire but when hitting the sack he had to wear a unique outfit. First he had a big cloth diaper taped on him, followed by a jumpsuit that zipped up at the back. This jumpsuit had very long sleeves. After getting zipped in, Peter would willingly put his arms straight out in front of himself so the long sleeves could be pulled through two thick plastic pipes. These pipes were slid up to his arm pits. The extra-long sleeves were then pulled back towards him covering the pipes all the way back to his armpits again and secured with strong fiber tape. This was done so Pete could not bend his elbows. As mentioned Pete seemed to happily submit to this form of restraint, then trot off to bed. When I asked what this was all about I was told, "That is how he came to us," meaning that was his bedtime routine when he came from Woodlands. I found out this contraption was to prevent Pete from smearing his feces at night.

The culture at Glendale was not the same as Woodlands but there were things that came with the folks transferred from there, including Pete's pipe restraints. I also realized that if you were new at Glendale, like at any job, you had to be careful how you questioned things. One might ask "Why do we do it that way?" The answer was usually, "That is the way we have always done it." Or when offering a different method or idea the answer would be, "We tried that 10 years ago. It didn't work."

My time came to do a month of the overnight shift. I arrived at 11p.m., said goodbyes to the afternoon shift and did my rounds where I checked out the 25 men. I walked past Pete's bed to see him still awake and attempting to scratch his nose by rubbing it against his piped arms. I got Pete to follow me to the bathroom to get him out of those restraints. I cut the fiber tape and wrestled the tubes off the sleeves. Pete was able to do the rest. I handed him a pair of blue polo pajamas and off he went to bed. That night worked out well. I did the same for the other 22 nights I worked that month. It was only on my last shift that I wrote a note about this successful experiment. The "tubing" restraint was eliminated. Having suggested this in a meeting with the higher ups it had a good chance of being shot down. "We tried that 10 years ago."

PULL MY FINGER

"A day without sunshine is like, you know, night."

Steve Martin

One of the things that was slow to change was the chain of command in a place like Glendale. The two departments that had the most clout were the nursing and psychology departments. With the nursing department most decisions were made with practical knowledge that affected their decisions. The psychology department not so much. The main reason for this was there were only a few of them and there were more than 325 people to help. Their ability to properly connect with all residents would be hard. Things could have improved by asking the hands-on staff before new ideas were implemented. There were times that we were asked for our input: however, I recollect very few of these recommendations being applied.

I did get a chance to have input regarding a resident with the psychology people. Before this encounter I had felt that after reading many of the behaviour plans handed down from their offices that they tended to lack much imagination. I am not at all suggesting that they meant any harm; on the contrary, they were doing what they thought was right based on what they had learned to get their qualifications. This academic information and theory, however, had little to do with the individuals they were hoping to help. It seemed to be directed towards changing their behaviour rather than trying to understand it. They either wanted to get them to do something or stop them from doing something.

Theories are big wide nets, meant to encompass the highest number of possibilities. For example, find out what the resident likes and when they do what you want, give them some reward. Smarties were the treat of choice at Glendale. If they have a possession they liked, take it away if the behaviour is not up to snuff. Most living in Glendale had no important possessions so one thing they all had was a tiny amount of freedom on the lodges. They could walk about, observe others and look out the window. A breach of proper behaviour resulted in a removal of freedom: time out. No looking out the window or observing others. They were isolated even more.

Very few of these behaviour programs were unique to the individual. How could they be unique regarding aggression when the only thing the psychologist knew was their behaviour? They did not have an experienced guess on what this behaviour may be communicating. To get this experience they had to know the person-form a relationship-if they wanted to better understand what made this person do the things he or she did. What made them tick?

There was little value placed on learning why residents of Glendale behaved the way they did. More importance was placed on eliminating that behavior. True understanding cannot be measured or quantified, but elimination can.

In Herbert Lovett's book, "Learning to Listen: Positive Approaches and People with Difficult Behaviour," he writes about it: *"There is no such thing as a value-free way of working with others. The challenge is to keep ourselves honest and to consider what values we actually use in our work and not just the values we say we use. One sad and painful ironies of psychology in the field of developmental disabilities is that we psychologists have judged (and often hurt) people on the basis of their observed behaviour. We, however, have overlooked, excused and even congratulated one another on the basis of our intentions."*

Walt was a new arrival to Glendale. This was in the mid-80s. At this time, new residents would only be admitted on an emergency basis. In Walt's case it was due to his threatening behaviour toward his house staff. Walt was a big, strong, athletic, young man, about 25 years old when I met him. He was well spoken, polite and inquisitive. He was confused as to why he was placed in Glendale. The official story was that Walt pulled a knife on his group home staff and threatened them with it. So seeing as Walt had a developmental disability Glendale was the place for him. I was lucky to be asked to be the one to spend time with him as we were about the same age and we both enjoyed being active. We would go to the small weight room at Glendale, as well as go for jogs and such. During our time together I asked Walt about what happened to get him sent to Glendale. He said he was in the kitchen making a sandwich and a staff was riding him hard about cleaning up. He yelled at them to leave him alone holding a butter knife in his hand. Walt, being a big guy, could be scary. So the cops were called and jail was not the place for him, Glendale was.

Walt was not happy at Glendale. We had some fun together but he missed his friends and his community. One afternoon during a walk with Walt along with a group from his lodge and another staff, he decided that he would go in a different direction than the rest of us were taking. He was heading down the one road away from Glendale. I told him that we were not going that way. He did not respond to me and kept walking. I ran to catch up with him while the other staff went back with the other residents. I asked where he was going." Home, I miss my friends," was his reply.

Good reasoning on his part I thought. I realized that he was determined to make the long trek and that there was no way I could physically stop him and bring him back; he must have outweighed me by 30 kilos. I did my best to try to bring some of the realities to his attention regarding his plan.

I told him that it would take days to get there as it was about a 300-kilometre walk. I went on to ask him where he would sleep, how would he eat and were would he get the money for the ferry ride needed to complete his goal of returning home. These problems did not seem to make much of a dint in his determination and off we continued. I decided to tell Walt that even though this was going to be a long trip that I would stay with him to keep him safe for as long as he continued this quest. I had already formed a relationship with him and felt I had built up trust between us and to threaten to leave him would have thrown that all away. What he needed was someone he could count on. He was scared and I told him that I understood his fear and I would help him though this.

While all this was going on the staff alerted the authorities in the building about this slow escape. Walt and I had walked about 5 kilometres when I noticed one of the Glendale vans following us at a distance. The driver had a walkie-talkie. It was what we used before cell phones. So with this device the driver could relay what was going on back to the mother ship. I would guess they were told to keep their distance so as not to spook Walt. This was a smart move on their part as Walt could have scooted into the bushes and we would have had a worse problem on our hands. Anyway, I was nearly out of reasoning on how he should abandon this plan and it was having little effect on his pace. Something inside of me made me come up with an idea and only part of it was from my brain. I asked Walt if he would stop for a moment. He obliged. When we stopped, the van stopped. The driver must have seen those spy movies: follow without being noticed. The van had Glendale in huge letters on the side so they were not fooling anyone. When we were stopped I asked Walt if he would pull my finger. He did. I then let go a big bark from my backside. Walt's face changed from serious and determined, to smiling. This juvenile comic distraction was what was needed for him. He had been listening to my words. He knew he would be on a long journey and the fart jolted him to that reality. We turned around and walked back to the van for the ride back to Glendale.

We were met upon arrival by one of the psychologists who seemed very anxious to pick my brain on how I was able to get Walt to abort his escape plan. This was a change in the norm, this department wanted to know something from me. My shift had already ended so it was decided that we would meet the next morning.

The next morning I entered the psychologist's office and we engaged in uncomfortable small talk-you know, the kind where someone is making an effort to show interest in what they think you are interested in, when it is clear that they have little concern or understanding of these interests. Anyway, after this small talk the questions came: "What did Walt and I talk about? How was his mood?" Then came the big question: "What did you do to get him to change his mind?" I replied "I made him laugh." Notes were taken. Then I was asked just how I made him laugh. Now with pen on paper waiting for my reply, I said, "I just asked him to pull my finger." This was written down promptly, then a looking up from the paper they asked, "then what?" I thought everybody knew what was going to happen when someone asks you to pull their finger. In this person's case I was mistaken. So I had to explain the pulling of the finger, then the simultaneous passing of gas, preferably in a loud fashion. There was a long pause accompanied by a puzzled look, then some writing. The last question asked was, "Which finger did he pull?" This was another indication that this psychologist had never experienced this form of immature humor before. I told them, it was my right index finger. Notes were written. I was thanked for my time and I left. I went away smiling with the thought that I as a lowly support worker was able to educate the educated. I mentioned that I thought the psychology department lacked imagination and I guess I can add it lacked a sense of humour as well.

BE IN MY SHOES

"You should never judge a person till you have walked a mile in their shoes. Then you can judge the hell out of them because ...well you're a mile away and they have no shoes."

Terry Flatt (stolen from some comedian)

To give an example of how, when you put yourself in the shoes of one you are supporting, you often gain an understanding on how best to provide that support. Walt would, whenever he felt that he had done something wrong or was chastised in anyway, lie down and curl up in the fetal position. It did not matter where he was, he would go down and stay there for hours. If it happened on his lodge it would be okay and we would just wait it out. On some occasions he would stay in this position for a long time and wet himself because he couldn't move until he went through what he needed to go through. If this would happen in public that was very inconvenient for me as I would have to inform people that he was not hurt and had some internal issues that had to be addressed and these issues take a bit of time.

A nurse asked me if I would come to a meeting with a person that she thought could help Walt with this problem and wanted my input. I was asked many questions and he then asked me if I could demonstrate this behaviour and be Walt during these times of shut downs. I was sceptical but agreed to do it.

I curled up in a ball on the office floor, closed my eyes and let this guy do his thing. His thing was to just talk to me softly, only saying positive things. He asks if he could rub my back, I don't reply as I was in character. I was determined to just lay there till he gave up. He continued to tell me that it was just fine that I was doing what I was doing. I continued to hang on tight to my thoughts of being Walt and this guy was not going to bring me out of it till I wanted to.

His voice was quiet and all he gave me was positive words and touch. I don't remember how long he was interacting with me but it was perhaps 10 minutes then I had to come out of it. I told the person that I did not want to have his positive words, soft tones and gentle touch affect me but they did. I asked him what would you have said if I had wet myself his reply was, "I would say;' that must feel better now to have let that come out," always positive."

When I was in the Walt character I believed him to be angry inside, angry at himself for doing wrong. I was thinking angry and I was trying hard to hang on to that anger.

I learnt that day that negative cannot live with positive for very long. This was a very powerful learning experience but I did not know how powerful it was at the time.

I continued to work with Walt and one day I said something that triggered this behaviour. We were loading a truck with yard waste and I corrected him in what I thought was a neutral way. He shut down. This was the first time since I had that lesson. It was near the end of my shift and I was angry inside that this could take a long time but I remember what I learnt. I did and said all the right things. To my surprise he was out for only 5 minutes, the fastest I experienced.

The next day I told everyone on the lodge this success and Walt's shut downs were short and with the positive talk, tone and touch, sweet.

BRENT'S REPUTATION

"Worry about your character, not your reputation. Your character is who you are. Your reputation is who people think you are."

John Wooden

My pal Brent, continued his, as recorded, aggressive ways. I had heard he was called "the million-dollar man" by the administration due to the compensation costs he caused. It was true that Brent was deemed responsible for many staff injuries. I, however, would like to argue that he could not take all the blame. I suggest that some staff received injuries while forcibly pulling him to the time-out room. I would say that this procedure, designed by the decision-makers, to demand the movement of an uncooperative person to isolation, led to back injuries. Perhaps if the policy was to have staff settle the situation where it happened, a percentage of injuries would have been avoided. Furthermore many reports would cite Brent for being "randomly aggressive", or would strike "for no apparent reason". My argument is that he had a reason. Now, I am not saying it was a good or noble reason, I am just saying that it was a reason for Brent. Where the system failed Brent was that in these situations few took the time to understand why he felt justified to attack. The focus was on the punishment or consequence of his actions. It was a wrongheaded thought that these punitive measures would have the effect of stopping his behaviours. One would think that looking for what triggers the behaviour might have been a worthwhile endeavor. It seemed that punishment won over prevention.

ENOUGH TO KNOCK OUT A HORSE

"The arrogant are wise in their eyes, but the wise will recognize their lies."

Unknown

There was plenty of wrongheaded decisions regarding Brent, one such example was with the new dentist. Glendale had a dental suite with all the dentistry bells and whistles. A dentist from the community would be hired on a contract basis, tending to the needs of the residents. There was a dental hygienist that worked full-time at Glendale and she was a wonderful human. I remember she would come onto the lodge flashing her big smile and her kind voice along with that smooth English accent. She had a calming effect on the residents as well as the staff. Her job was to help where she could with the teeth and gum care and then ascertain the procedures that needed the expertise of a dentist. So when she accumulated enough of those in need of a higher level of attention the community dentist would be called.

It was well known that Brent did not do well with any dentist. Not sure why but I would guess it would be due to a Woodlands experience. The hygienist suggested, for good reason, that Brent be put under a general anaesthetic to have a cleaning and some cavities filled. This dentist disregarded her recommendation and decided to simply prescribe pills to make Brent sleep. I was called to help deliver him to the dentist. I arrived on Brent's lodge to find him sound asleep in a wheelchair. I brought along another male staff to deliver Brent to the dentist and transfer him to the dentist chair. Even as lowly staff we knew this was a bad idea. We wheeled the sleeping Brent into the dental suite. The dentist was getting things prepared and in a condescending master/servant tone, he told us to put Brent in the dental chair. I suggested to the dentist that there was a chance that this could go sideways as in the past he was always put out for these things. I was immediately told, "I prescribed enough dope to knock out a horse." He could have been right about the dosage and what it would do to a horse but as it turned out it was not enough to knock out Brent. We lifted a sleeping Brent from the wheelchair and as soon as his ass hit the dentist chair one eye opened and Brent, with what seemed like pinpoint accuracy, booted the dentist right in the chops. This blow split his bottom lip and then this clearly over-confident doctor yelled, "get him out of here," as he turned to focus on his wound. We lifted Brent back to the wheelchair where he calmly went back to sleep. Such was the hierarchy of institutions: those in the higher pay scale knew better, front line workers were there to be told what to do and how to do it. Questioning them, well, that was out of the question.

AUTHORITY, I QUESTION YOU

"When the power of love overcomes the love of the power, the world will know peace."

Jimi Hendrix

There were others working at Glendale that thought very highly of themselves. They were happy to let you know their place in the pecking order and liked to remind you of your place.

I, like Brent, did not take kindly to others being less than kind or disrespectful. I had a charge nurse, in an authoritative tone, tell me to stop the task I was doing and tend to something else. I said that she could have asked me nicely. Her reply was "I don't have time to be nice." My retort was, "Well you seemed to be able to find the time to be rude." I said this in a friendly joking tone along with a smile. I will take a rude shot but I will sarcastically give one back. One should not pitch if they are not ready to catch.

There are few things that piss me off and one of them is some flag persons. You know the people who hold signs to stop you during road construction. Now I understand the need for me to stop. I know that I have to take my turn and let the other drivers opposite to me be on their way in an orderly fashion. I have no problem with that. What I do have a problem with is when they do so without a smile or eye contact. If someone is going to tell me what to do I would like it to be done nicely. In the world of persons with developmental disabilities, they are told what to do for almost all their awake hours.

So knowing how I react inside to some flag people I am very careful to be as nice as possible when I ask or tell someone what to do. It takes the same amount of time and energy and the reality is that you get better results.

There was a time, actually a few times, where I got in trouble with a person of authority at Glendale. This one is an example of when I questioned said authority.

I rode my bike to work in those days and would chain it to these brown metal supports that held up the second floor balconies. Another staff alerted me that Mr. Simms (not his real name) had placed a note on the seat of my bike. I quickly collected said note and it read as such: Please do not lock your bike to these poles. Your security chain will chip the paint off these poles and we will have to paint them before it is necessary.

This man was a person who had his own office, he had little contact with those who lived at Glendale and mostly paid attention to the staff and any of their indiscretions on where they parked their cars or bikes.

I did some thinking about the note and its directive. I came up with a reply. I used an inter-departmental memo to pass along my thoughts. This memo was like a postcard, not private: the person delivering could, and I would guess, often read them. The memo I sent read something like this- Re: My chain chipping the paint. I know you are a busy person, with plenty to do here at Glendale. This is probably why you did not notice the plastic coating on my security chain. This plastic coating would be hard- pressed to chip the paint you are worried about. I hope that this knowledge of the plastic coating will alleviate your important and real concerns.

I may have gone over the top and it was many years ago and perhaps those were not the exact words I used but you get my drift. I was not very concerned about the repercussions but I knew it would stir things up. That memo had the desired effect. He came stomping into the nursing office and being shift change it, was full of staff.

He said in a very loud and commanding voice, "Terry we need to talk," I said "Sure Mike, where?" He replied "that's Mr. Simms to you." I said "Then it's Mr. Flatt to you." He told me to go to the empty meeting room down the hall. We got to the room and he directed me to enter first. I decline this offer and suggest that he enter first. We were at a stalemate and I insisted it's only gentlemanly of me. He finally went in, I followed and he went back to the door and slammed it for effect. He then ordered me to sit down. I told him that I would rather stand, this shouldn't take long. Then in a very quiet and inquisitive way I asked, "What seems to be the problem?"

I noticed a change in his demeanour, he seemed less confident. He went on to say what his problem was, "I didn't like that sarcastic comment in that memo of me being a busy person." He was kind of vibrating with perhaps anger or unsure of what he was going to say next. I then in a very Dalai Lama tone said, "Oh, I am sorry you took what I wrote as being sarcastic for it was not my intention, aren't you a busy person?"

This was when he sat down and started to ramble about how he used to ride to work and something about different types of bike locks on the market. I could see that he was at a loss of what to say or do. He wanted out of this situation; his attempt at intimidation did not have the affect he wanted. I did not react the way he had expected. He did not have a plan for me not being intimidated. I helped him out by saying that I think we are done here and thanks for the chat. He seemed to leave flustered. I left smiling. I learned a good lesson that day that helped me when I became a contractor and an advocate for persons with developmental disabilities.

After this incident I had another authoritative encounter with this individual. It was in the cafeteria. Administration would have their lunch break after the direct support staff were finishing up theirs. I was carrying my empty lunch dishes on a tray and walked past a table full of these administrative folks when he piped up to me and said that I was in violation of the dress code. I stopped and ask what this violation was. He informed me that if a staff were to wear shorts, the hem must be three inches above the knee. I was wearing rugby shorts with an elastic waist band. I placed down my tray and proceeded to hike my shorts down so the hem met the dress code requirements. This led to the top of my shorts now covering only part of my backside. I picked up the tray and on my way out half mooned the cafeteria. I expected another visit for being cheeky, (pun intended,) but I suppose he thought twice about it seeing as the last meeting did not go the way he had envisioned.

THE MAGIC WORDS OF THE HOUSEKEEPER

"Life's most persistent and urgent question is, what you are doing for others."

Martin Luther King, Jr.

There were a bunch of other people working at Glendale who did not have hands-on contact with those living there. I have called Glendale "the big house," but it was not a house in most person's eyes. However, according to the Oxford English Dictionary: "house; a building for human habitation; a building in which animals live or in which things are kept." I would think for Glendale, both definitions had a ring of truth.

There were many departments that kept the building running. Dietary, laundry and housekeeping. Workers from these areas had uniforms that could tell us what department they worked in. These staff had some contact with those living there and some of those staff had more than others. The department that had the best ability to forge relationships with the residents were the housekeeping people. There was one housekeeper per lodge. They would keep the floors, bathrooms and windows clean. More often than not they had a good understanding of the goings-on with regards to those living there.

This brings me to Margret. She was Lodge Two's housekeeper. A wonderful woman, she would have been in her late 50s early 60s and she was one of those who was at Glendale from the start. She saw her lodge fill up with the 25 men who lived there.

There was nothing in her job description that would involve the care of the residents, other than to report things she should report such as abuse or injuries. The physical and emotional well-being of the guys on Lodge two was the responsibility of the HCWs, the Health Care Workers like myself.

Margret was working for 10 years on the lodge before I showed up. During those 10 years she formed a special relationship with Larry. Larry was a big, gentle guy who had average vocabulary along with frequent seizures. One would see Margret and Larry walking, or in Larry's case shuffling down the hallway together as they went to the cafeteria during her coffee break. This was not unheard of by the housekeeping staff, to have a special relationship with a person on the lodge they worked, but Larry and Margret were unique.

There were some things going on with Larry. It was noticed that his behaviour was changing. He was becoming more withdrawn, less talkative and such. This observation led to a scheduled meeting with the psychology folks. We had just had the "old-school" charge nurse retire and we got a progressive open-minded new charge nurse as his replacement. If I had suggested that Margret attend this meeting to the old nurse it would have been shot down. After I told this new guy about the relationship those two had he said, sure, why not?

I was at the meeting along with Margret, other lodge staff and the psychologist. This psychologist seemed confused that Margret was at the table but when it was explained that she had known Larry for over 15 years she was accepted as a contributor to the meeting. Contribute she did.

You see, Margret was off work for about a month and had a few more weeks of recovery due to an operation and so the coffee and conversation with Larry stopped. She was still off work but came in for the meeting. She suggested that he was just sad; he missed his friend. She suggested that during what was left in her absence, a staff that knew Larry well should keep up this ritual. She said that, "The staff should engage in conversation with Larry during these times and do more listening, even if they did not completely understand what he was saying. Just let him talk." What great insight to this problem, and what a great solution. It was implemented and an improvement was noticed right away. In less enlightened circumstances a happy pill would have been prescribed and that would have been that.

Without Margret attending that meeting, more dope would have been the solution.

Larry did not care about Margret's position or her job description. He cared about their relationship and he cared about her. She was allowed to speak up at the meeting and she was heard. This was not only for the benefit of Larry; it had an effect on the hands-on staff. We learned how powerful a little bit of listening was.

THIS IS BETWEEN HIM AND ME

"The less we try to control the chaos, the more at peace we are with the madness."

Madalyn Beck

I continued to bump into Brent from time to time and in this particular instance it was a hard bump indeed. I was working on his lodge and was helping him with his bath. He needed assistance getting in and out of the tub as well as paying attention to all the sweet spots. Like most of us he enjoyed his time in the tub. I was having a conversation with him, or perhaps it would better be described that I was listening to the conversation he was having with himself. Anyway, he was in a fine mood, no signs of agitation. I thought it was a good idea to prepare Brent for what was next on the agenda. As I was helping him from the tub I told him that I would get him in his pajamas, then get his teeth brushed. Like the dentist, I never saw it coming: POW, I received a sock to the jaw. I guessed he was loading up for another so I spun this still damp man around so the offending fist was not facing me. Then I wrapped my arms around him, holding him, his back to my front. I was confident I had the dangerous parts contained then BOOM he throws his head back hitting me in the temple and causing me to see stars. I did not let go of my hug but fell backward onto the floor, with my body cushioning Brent's fall. There we were, my back on the floor, Brent on top of me still working on a way to get free and cause me more harm. I say this because while I was holding him in this position he was very coherently telling me how my death was going to happen soon and he would be the one responsible for it. I had positioned myself to be out of range of another head butt and his arms were secured. I then started to talk calmly to him. You see I was a young fellow, mid 20s and had played rugby and hockey. I have experience with physical contact and was not upset or mad at Brent. I knew this was part of the game. I also knew that fighting fire with fire is such a stupid plan. Brent would be cursing me and I would be responding with calm talk, telling him that I would let him go if he promised not to hit me again. I would hold him with only the force needed to prevent a hit. I wanted him to know I didn't want to hurt him.

I knew I was making progress with him as his struggling was slowing down, as were his angry words. It was then that another staff came in the bathroom, seeing a naked wet Brent on top of me while I was holding him and calmly talking to him. This staff asked if I needed any help, I said, "This is between him and me, I will be fine," and he left believing I had things under control. I did not want protocol to kick in. This would have meant a bunch of staff would hold his arms and legs, then he would be transferred to the isolation room. I felt I was making headway with him and this type of time-out intervention would have been helpful to no one. I think that when Brent realised that I had no ill will toward him and that I was not going to give to him what he gave to me, he started to settle. I again said calmly that if he would promise not to hit me I would let him go. I gave him plenty of time to answer; I did not rush him. I knew he understood what I said. We lay in this position for at least five minutes, I would gradually loosen my hold to show my goodwill and finding less of an effort to hit when doing so. Brent finally said, "I promise." I was still a bit concerned that he was playing me so I said, "You promise what?" "Not to hit you," was his reply. We untangled ourselves and got on with the process of getting ready for bed. I made no mention of the incident on record, fearing reprisal for not following protocol.

I did not realize it at the time that this experience would be the foundation of a wonderful relationship.

A MOTHERS LOVE

"Family means no one gets left behind, or forgotten."

David Ogden Stiers

When Brent was in Woodlands his mother visited as often as she could but the distance and costs caused these visits to be less than she would have liked. When Brent moved to Glendale and his mom was in the same city the visits became more frequent. Almost every time she would visit she would bring him a present, often clothes. In Glendale most residents did not have clothes of their own. "Ward stock," as it was called, were interchangeable things to wear. When putting the "bundle"-the clothing to be worn the next day-staff would choose attire that would fit the person the bundle was intended for. Brent however had a section of his own because his mom would have his name stitched in everything she brought.

These visits did not always go well. Brent would be loaded with many frustrations in his day-to-day life and when his mother came to visit, he sometimes would not be shy in taking these frustrations out on her. One afternoon I was the escort for one of these visits. We met at a park. My job was to intervene if Brent became aggressive toward her. On this afternoon he was in a great mood. Brent's mom loved her son and had great expectations for him. Some of her hopes could be described as unrealistic. On that afternoon she said to me "When Brent becomes better and he gets his driver's license I will buy him a convertible because he loves the wind in his hair." I found this to be beyond the realm of possibilities but I could see that she saw something in Brent that no one else could see. A mother's love allows her to see her children differently than others; her wishes for her son become her focus even if they were unrealistic. Her love for Brent and her belief that he was going to get better was so strong it pushed the boundaries of reality. Who was I to tell her that her dreams for her son would not come true; no one has the right to step on those dreams. In years to come I and others were able to witness what his mother was able to see in Brent. I should note that no one would think that Brent would one day get his license and drive a car but some saw that there was more to him than his aggression. Most, however, at Glendale could not look past his reputation and believed him to be nothing more than dangerous.

Brent's brother and sister had little to do with him when he moved to Glendale and this was not only because they both had young families and careers but also because their mother discouraged them from visiting him. I suspect she wanted to spare them the emotional, and at times physical, hurt of seeing their brother living this way.

THE PROMISE KEYS

"Don't give up. Normally it is the last key on the ring that opens the door."

Paulo Coelho

In 1986 I took off to do some traveling to South East Asia. I was gone for a little less than a year and upon my return I applied to work at Glendale again. I was hired immediately.

Not much had changed at Glendale until I saw Brent. Turns out the seclusion plan had little to no effect on reducing his aggression. In the attempt to keep staff safe from Brent the next thing in the tool box was chemical restraint. They decided to dope him up to the point that he was unsteady on his feet, so much so he had to get around in a wheelchair. He was restrained in the chair to prevent him from getting up, then falling down. As with the dentist incident, the drugs had little effect on his aggression toward staff. What it did was frustrate him even more by taking away part of his ability to walk. It also made his targets closer; when the staff were moving him around in his chair, they were within striking distance. Brent became adapt at the backward swing, catching unsuspecting staff pushing the wheelchair.

Brent's frustration level was so high and his anger was so intense that management decided to implement one-to-one staffing on a two hour rotation. This was thought to be a way to avoid staff burnout. This also meant that Brent saw a new, reluctant, and often scared staff every two hours. This procedure was going on for a few months before I was put in the rotation.

With my first stint with Brent, I saw a very angry man. The woman I was replacing seemed extremely happy to see me. She had done the morning routine and breakfast with him. My two hours were the downtime between meals. When I walked into the room I was unsure if Brent would remember me from the bath-time incident. He did. I would like to say he became calm and happy upon my arrival. He didn't. The person I replaced could not get out of there fast enough. You see, when you are always afraid of getting hit, and the person you are afraid of is constantly talking negatively, it takes an emotional toll.

Brent could read people's emotions; he knew how you felt about him. It became my belief that if you showed that you were afraid of him he was distrustful of you. I was not afraid of Brent. Don't get me wrong, I'm no masochist, I just had confidence in my ability to get out of the way, albeit our bath time tussle might seem otherwise. I also had confidence in my ability to reach Brent with not only my words but how I said those words: my tone would be sincere, and I would react to his negative talk with positive responses. I would not be dragged into his negativity, I would coax him out of his pessimism with being upbeat and really listening to what he was saying. Brent is smart and plenty of what he was saying had meaning, certainly meaning to him.

Most people thought the things Brent talked about were gibberish, streams of consciousness seemingly going nowhere. He had something to say and most people in his life did not bother to listen. My guess is this was one of the reasons for his frustrations, leading to anger, then aggression. Not unlike citizens that revolt against their governments, these people feel they are not being listened to, they are not being heard. Lack of respect and lack of listening can and does lead people to violence with or without a developmental disability.

The French philosopher Emanuel Levinas thought that human interactions are the basis of personal ethics. He suggested that listening gives rise to empathy which, in turn, gives our lives meaning and direction. Listening to others reminds us of our human fragility and it helps others, to believe that we will do them no harm. When we engage with a person, our behavior will help or hinder our understanding of the person thereby it will strengthen or weaken that relationship. Listening will almost always help our understanding and can be the foundation of a stronger relationship. Henry David Thoreau wrote, "The greatest compliment that was ever paid to me was when someone asked me what I thought, and attended to my answer." Brent, during our early interaction, never asked me what I thought but I would always try to be attentive to his thoughts, his words. Listening is a courtesy and more important it is a sign of respect. You can't convince someone that you respect them by saying the words. You must show them respect and listening is the best way to do that.

So Brent and I became re-acquainted, I wheeled him about, we headed outside to enjoy the sun, I listened to his talk and responded when I would catch something I understood. His talk started to move away from negative. He stopped calling me an asshole and he was way more settled than when I first saw him that morning. So "nourishment" time rolled around, when the residents got a snack between meals and it was also the time I was to be relieved. We headed back to the lodge and in the dining room I saw the woman who was sent to replace me, or at least I thought that is why she was there. When I asked, she replied in a very unenthusiastic way that yes, indeed, she was my replacement. I asked if she would rather go back to her lodge and I would do her two-hour stint. This time she said, "Yes" with enthusiasm. She buggered off very quickly as if to get out of there before I could change my mind. Such was the effect Brent was then having on staff.

Nourishment over, Brent and I went wandering the hallways of Glendale. We came upon an abandoned lodge. Downsizing, as it came to be called, had been happening and one lodge was empty. This lodge then became a kind of activity area: floor-hockey sticks and net and some balls and such. We arrived and the place was all ours.

I kicked a few balls around then Brent said to me in a very clear voice, "your keys" and with my practice of interacting verbally with Brent when he said something that I understood, I asked what he meant. He said, "Give me your keys." My first thought was no way, I would never get them back. I then remembered our altercation during bath time and how he kept his promise not to hit me. Brent was tethered to his chair and I knelt down, put my hands on his knees and said "only if you promise to give them back when I ask for them." I took them off my belt and had them in my hands. Brent's eyes did not leave the keys. I asked again, "Do you promise to give them back?"

He said, "Yes, I promise," but I still was unsure; getting them back could mean a huge confrontation and I wanted to avoid that. I also wanted Brent to trust me and the best way to get that was to trust him. I then said to Brent, "Yes, you promise to do what?" His reply was "give back the keys," but he said that without taking his eyes off them. I asked him again and I asked him to look in my eyes and say it. This took a few minutes, then he said, while looking at me, "I promise to give the keys back." So, still a bit apprehensive, I untied him from the chair and gave him my keys. I decided that if I wanted him to believe me I had to believe him.

He held them for a moment, just staring at them. Brent could walk, albeit a bit unsteady and slowly due to the large amount of drugs he was on. He was equipped with a hockey helmet for protection in case of a tumble, so I helped him out of his chair and walked around the empty lodge with him. I showed him the one key that would open most doors on any lodge; it was called the "40 key", as it had a "40" stamped on it. I have a vivid memory of how slowly and precisely he inserted the key, then with a quick twist the door was opened. He went outside and closed the door, then proceeded to open it again, come inside, close it, and then repeat.

This must have been a magic time for him. For years he watched staff come and go as they pleased. A door to them was not a wall as it was to Brent and for all who lived on a locked lodge. Keys or at least the possession of them was a freedom tool and now they were in his hands. After a few minutes of opening and closing the day-room door Brent turned his attention to the nursing office. This was a room, on all lodges, where charts, records and such were kept, and where the staff met. This room had three big windows, so while in that office, staff could have a good view of the goings-on in the large rooms. This was a room that most residents saw only from the outside with noses pressed up against the glass. When Brent got to the office door he hesitated and again took his time. When he did open it, he slowly walked in and he said "he's in, he's in." This was the calmest I had ever seen him of late. His talk was mostly about the keys and the doors.

Brent walked around the lodge exploring and talking to himself. Now the time came to prepare to get the keys back. I started the warnings early, "you have 10 minutes; and then I get the keys back." I would get no response from him but I knew he heard and understood me. I gave him the five-minute warning, then two, then it was time. I walked up to him and I could see, by the look on his face and by his hand tightening around the keys, that this might be a chore to get the keys back. I said, "I need the keys back Brent." He squeezed them tighter. I used soft talk, told him we could do this again, but not unless I got them back now. I was getting close to thinking I would have to take them by force. I tried one more time with a twist. I asked him "I need the promise keys back." His eyes, were squinting at the keys, opened wide and, to my surprise, he handed them back. A promise clearly meant something to him, I know it did.

I explained to Brent that we would come back after lunch and play with the doors. I thought about telling the higher-ups about what we had just done but decided not to. I had the fear that they would put an end to this experiment.

Off we went to have lunch and again I sent the relief staff away. Brent and I went back to the abandoned lodge and played with the doors some more and when the time came to ask for the keys back there was no problem getting them returned.

I did not tell those above me but I did tell Rex, the guy replacing me when my shift was over. Rex also had a good understanding of Brent and like me was not afraid of him. I told Rex he should volunteer for the whole shift. Before I left I asked the charge nurse if I could do the entire shift the next day with Brent and she agreed, as she knew this gig was not one others wanted. Rex did the same for the afternoon shift. We did this for a few months, Brent playing with the doors and enjoying the power of the keys. We were able to get two more guys on board with doing the "promise keys," so most days were covered for Brent.

Alas, all things come to an end, and so was my time working at Glendale. The move of the Glendale residents to the community was going at a good pace. Group homes were set up, mostly four to a house. Day programs were needed to give those in the homes something meaningful to do with their days. There was a need for me to think about my future employment. I started a non-profit society, submitted a proposal to operate a day program that would support folks coming out of Glendale. It was accepted and I was out of the big house. Brent stayed.

GOOD PEOPLE IN A BAD SYSTEM

"If you don't like something change it. If you can't change it, change your attitude."

Mya Angelo

Before I leave Glendale I must say a few positive things about the place. It is hard to find positive things about a place that warehoused people but I can describe some of the good people who worked in a less- than- good system.

John: He worked with Brent and was one of the few people who saw Brent as more than just a behaviour. John also thought outside the box-the box being the Glendale building. Glendale was located away from the public eye and surrounded by fields and woods. In the woods there was an old trail that was in bad shape. This was due to the huge parking lot built for the staff cars and the water runoff was the reason for a very soggy section of the trail. John and his band of residents of Lodge six would, between meals, head to the trail, maintenance tools in hand, to do the needed upkeep. Residents who never had an opportunity to do something with a purpose apart from bed-making, table-setting or taking out the laundry bags, now had something meaningful to do with their time, almost all of the "jobs" residents had at Glendale were inside jobs.

John changed that for some. These men, who almost certainly were taught to walk in an institution, had little experience walking on uneven ground. John and his trail crew got away from the walls and halls of Glendale. If only for a few hours a day, it was more than they had before John came along.

Joyce: What a lovely woman…unless you crossed her. The way to cross her was to give less than great care for those living on her lodge.

I was a young guy, full of fun, carefree, always joking and Joyce was okay with that. She was and is a fun person herself. She, however, was dead serious when it came to advocating for those she supported. Joyce worked on an extended-care lodge. These residents needed total personal care.

I was a relief staff one evening on Joyce's lodge and we were in the bathroom giving folks their evening baths. There were two tubs in close proximity and I was bathing Rick. Joyce and I were going about our business when she raised her voice and said, "That is not the way you clean a foreskin!" She was watching me the whole time and caught me doing an inadequate job. I was a bit taken aback by this but realized she was not being bossy, she was paying attention. She cared about her people; they were important to her and anyone who was going to provide support for them had better do it the right way.

There were many people who were like Joyce working at Glendale but she was one of a kind. We became good friends after my attempt at a shortcut on proper penis cleaning. She was a mother bear for those in her care.

There were many who deserve recognition but the last person was Robert: He was a guy with a tie-aka management: Nursing management, to be more precise. He was a friend to those living at Glendale and those working there. He was at every planning meeting regarding a resident. He knew everybody and their stories. Robert was well respected and was the glue that held the place together. I watched as he interacted with the residents. He conversed with them even if they could not talk. He made the biggest impact on me with regards to how I would connect with those living at Glendale.

I was at his celebration of life and his son talked about how his dad's second family were those living at Glendale. His son recalled how, soon after the Christmas presents were opened, his dad would be off to Glendale and back for dinner that night. I worked a few Christmas days and Robert would come to every lodge and did not miss a resident or staff with a heartfelt handshake or a hug and a cheery Merry Christmas. A great guy who made life the best he could for those in that big house.

FROM GLENDALE TO COMMUNITY

"If you don't like the road you are walking, start paving another one."

Dolly Parton

William was a Woodlands survivor who followed the same path as Brent. He was a small man who had learned how to survive in the old institution and would have found the new digs at Glendale to be a positive shift. Willy was not a big fan of change so when things were being set up for his new home in the community he was reluctant to leave. My guess was that having a bunch of new staff in his life frightened him. This changeover took time. He would not get into the community van. He would, however, happily get into the Glendale van, which he was used to. Willy would visit the house to have lunch or dinner with his roommates but when the meal was over he wanted to go back to Glendale. His fear of this change was understandable. We all fear the unknown. His first sleepover did not go well: he would not sleep, have a bath or get into pajamas. I was told that the next night was more successful and I suspect that after spending a few nights at his community home without anything bad happening his fears were diminished.

I worked with Willy in his new day program during this time. After he had settled into his new home we went to Glendale for a party, but Willy refused to get out of the van. I think he had made the decision that his new small home was better than Glendale, his old big one.

Not all the information moved with those leaving Glendale. Although there were files on the residents, history, date of birth and such but their personal preferences were not always included in these notes. The experienced caregivers at Glendale would verbally pass on these preferences to new staff and this information might not be put in the file. Such was the case with Paul, who did not talk but had strong likes. One of these preferences was not forwarded to the new staff at his home. I found this out at a chance meeting with one of his home staff. I asked how Paul was doing and she told me that he was doing well for the most part. Turns out that he would sometimes, for no reason they could see, have this huge freak-out when bed time rolled around. The freak-outs went something like this: he would tear up his pajamas and pee on them, all the while screaming. I had worked with Paul and asked what type of pajamas they had at the house. She replied that he had the same polo pajamas that he came with from Glendale. These pajamas came in two colours: brown and blue. For some reason it was not conveyed that Paul liked blue and the staff had a 50/50 chance of getting him the right ones. She was thrilled with this bit of information and I am sure Paul was as well.

I'M OUT, BRENT STAYS

"Life is a journey which never lets you know when and where it will end."

Biju Karakkonam

As mentioned, I did some traveling. I did the backpack thing through all the drug-producing countries in Southeast Asia. Nepal was my favorite country. While trekking the hills the locals would greet tourists with, "Namaste". I did not know the word before but I found out that it meant, "Hello." The real translation was, "I salute the divine qualities within you." Upon my return to Canada I started my plans to develop a non-profit society and operate a day program for those coming out of Glendale. I had the name for the society: Namaste. It fit my belief that those we support have divine qualities within them.

Now I was working in the community with a brand-new non-profit society and formed a day program and had 11 ex-Glendale residents to support. I was out of Glendale, Brent was not. Plans were made for those leaving Glendale to be placed in homes willy-nilly throughout the community. The way it seemed to work was those thought to be easier to support, in the behavioural sense, were placed first. The homes were mostly four people under the same roof. Day programs were needed and the numbers attending these programs were around 10 to 15. One would hope that the staff who cared for these folks at Glendale would move with them to their homes and day programs but this was rarely the case. The reason? Wages. Those working at

Glendale were unionized and classified as government employees. The jobs in the community were not classified as government jobs and the long-time Glendale staff had the option to transfer to other positions in the government, keep their wages and benefits and continue to pay into their pensions. The wages in the community were almost half that of Glendale and the benefits were none. Glendale staff did help with the set-up and training, but they could not afford to switch to day program or home workers at such a huge pay cut and complete loss of benefits. The people who came in to fill these community positions did their best to form the much-needed relationships to transition residents from Glendale to a world they were kept out of for most of their lives.

This was a unique time as most of the new staff had little or no experience with supporting these particular persons with developmental disabilities. For these folks coming out of Glendale they had to get to know almost all new staff and a new environment.

During these busy times of change, Brent's world began to shrink. He was not seen as a good fit in a home. All those caregivers involved with the "promise keys" were gone, transferred to other government jobs or a job in a home or day program in the community. Rex stayed the longest but he eventually had to jump the sinking Glendale ship to secure employment elsewhere. This left Brent surrounded by strangers who were afraid of him, so his frustration escalated along with his aggressive behaviour. Meanwhile, I was merrily running a day program and had no knowledge, and I feel bad about this, I made no enquiries on how he was doing. It would be five years before I would see Brent again.

During these five years the Namaste day program was chugging along. Our program started in January, 1992, near the end of the downsizing process. As mentioned, those without behavioural issues went first so our "grouping," as it was called, was 11 men from Glendale, almost all with a history or reputation of aggression or challenging behaviour. We were up to the task of supporting these guys using the things that I learnt from Brent: listen to their words and behaviour to better understand what their problems are. We soon became the go-to place for others who, for behavioural reasons, did not fit where they were placed. Our numbers went to 15 in a few years.

BRENT IS THE LAST TO GO

"People who look down on other people don't end up being looked up to."

Robert Hall

In 1997 I received a call from Dave, an ex-charge nurse from Glendale, asking me for some help in writing a plan to give to a potential residential service provider for Brent to move into the community. He called me because he knew I had success with Brent in Glendale. I told him two main things, treat him with respect and don't be afraid of him. Well, that was the short version of what I said.

Dave and I met to discuss Brent's support plan further with the social worker in charge of Brent's release from Glendale. Turns out, it was only Brent residing there. Due to Brent's reputation for aggression, he did not have community residential service providers rushing to provide support for him. How could you blame them as the homes were all set up and running well. To throw Brent into the mix had the potential, literally, of knocking things off kilter. A home share was set up for Brent but that did not end well. Then one brave organization said they would give it a try, but only after they received a support plan

At this meeting with Dave and the ministry social worker, I was asked to write a potential support plan for Brent and submit it to the social worker by the end of the week. I said I would be delighted to. After the meeting I asked Dave what he was charging for writing Brent's support plan. He told me, so I charged half of what he was charging. I was not very experienced at this type of thing so I took considerable time in explaining the main things I felt were needed in his support plan: staff need to show respect for Brent and not be afraid of him. I handed in my support plan, along with an invoice for my time at our next scheduled meeting with the social worker. I was gobsmacked when the social worker told me, "I asked if you would do it. I never said I would pay you for it." I filed this away in the "now I know" category when dealing with this ministry and this social worker.

So Brent moved into his new home with his reputation leading the way. Hindsight is clear, but this organization did not stand a chance. Brent was coming from a place that was not having success supporting him and these unsuccessful ways of understanding Brent came along with him, firmly attached to his dangerous classification. This house was set up under one roof but with Brent's area separated from the main house by a locked door.

The staff of, "the pink house," as Brent came to call it, were great people. They were supporting others with high needs, they had good skills and were very professional. When it came to supporting Brent they were given poor information. They were given only a one-dimensional picture of who Brent was. These staff were, and properly so, warned about his aggression and his long experience and skill at injuring staff. These workers were trained to fear him, the opposite of the training I suggested. No wonder I did not get paid for my plan; they had no intention of using it. The other part of my suggested support strategy was the need to show Brent respect, respect for being smart, and respect for having something to say. They must also respect what he says. I suspect the thing they were taught to respect was his ability to hurt them. It is hard to respect a person as a person when you are scared of him.

The plan was to have an in-house day program for Brent as the ministry felt that there was no community-run day support that would have him. I was told by the pink house staff that he arrived like a whirling dervish, the Bug's Bunny cartoon Tasmanian devil. Brent had left a place where he was misunderstood to join another place of misguided, albeit good, people. The staff were given the skills of defending themselves from injury but no insight into the whole person that Brent was.

Brent's aggression and agitation was taking its toll on the pink house staff. It wasn't long before I received a call from the social worker that stiffed me on my support plan. He asked me about the possibility of Brent coming to our day program. I jumped at the chance. I was told that Brent would come with one-to-one funding, so off I went to find Rex. As luck would have it Rex was just ending a contract and was about to go looking for other work. We were set: Brent would be supported by at least two guys that had a positive past relationship with him. It goes without saying but I will say it anyway, you can't have a good relationship with a person without understanding who this person is. Rex and I had had such an understanding.

Brent was coming to a program that was supporting three other men who he had lived with at Glendale, so there was familiarity for sure. This was set up fast as the turmoil at the pink house was very much in need of relief. We had little preparation time but we were ready: we had two staff who respected Brent and were not afraid of him.

Brent arrived at 9 a.m. on a Monday and the whirling dervish came out of the pink house van. Rex and I were shocked at what we saw. Brent's eyes were on fire. He was as angry as I had ever seen him. He had either not been prepared by the home staff or he was too angry to understand where he was going. Brent looked up and saw both of us and I would like to say he smiled and gave us a big hug…but such was not the case. His agitation was so high his awareness of his surroundings seemed limited. As it was five years since I last saw him and three years for Rex, I thought perhaps he forgot who we were. Brent came charging up to us. The home staff thought it aggressive but Rex and I knew otherwise. Brent grabbed Rex's hand and said "Rexman, get him a coffee" as Brent will refer to himself in the third person. Rex said, "Sure," and off they went to the day-program house. A coffee was poured and Brent slowly settled with Rex by his side. I came into the house after explaining to the house staff that we had a handle on him. I arrived at the table with Rex and Brent. Brent looked over at me and said "Flattie, how about the promise keys." Brent obviously remembered Rex and me. I told Brent I would see what I could do. That day, Rex took Brent out in his car and although Brent had settled from a 10 down to a 5, he was still agitated. As Rex had the two main tools needed, the day went well. Brent's home van arrived at 3:00 and it was apparent to Brent he was heading back to a place where people did not understand him. He went up to 10 in agitation. The next morning was much the same; high upon arrival, then some settling after time with people whom he trusted. That morning I had put together a set of keys on a ring that resembled the Glendale promise keys. I gave them to Brent and just like the time I got Brent the white sheet at Glendale, nary a thank you. I was okay with that, placing an importance on politeness was not the immediate goal. Having the keys in his hands seemed to mitigate his anger somewhat. It was not the magic pill I was hoping for, but it did seem to calm him down. We had some minor incidents over the next few weeks, but nothing of much significance.

So Brent had his keys but he was only allowed to have them at the program as the pink house did not want them to come home with him. They thought he would use them as a weapon. While at the day program Brent took a shine to a yellow rain slicker: he called it a "jacket raincoat." Brent wanted to wear it and seeing no harm in this we allowed him to put it on. We saw this new possession of his as a good thing. When the time came for him to head back to the pink house he did not want to take the coat off. I told the home staff it was okay with me if he took it with him. The staff said, "Oh no, he can't have the jacket." I thought I was unclear and said again that indeed he could take it home; it was fine with me. The reply was that if he took it home then he would fixate on it. I said, "I got a hot tip for you he-already is and if you let him have it then that fixation will go away." Turns out this reasoning did not fly at the pink house. I was also told that if Brent got what he wanted that would spoil him. That reasoning eluded me. He was not asking for something that would be in the spoiling category. It was a jacket: something we all had and at times needed. Turns out it was his ability to choose the jacket that was the issue. Brent could have a jacket-it just had to be one that the staff had chosen or deemed appropriate. I argued a little but soon realized Brent would have to leave his choice of attire behind. It was clear to me that the fight to control Brent in all aspects of his life, was one of the main causes of their problems with him.

Rex and I were skilled enough to deflect, re-direct or just take the time to listen to any words or actions that we could use to connect with Brent in his world. Brent taught me years ago that it is way easier to try to get into his world than to attempt to force him into mine. I said it was easier, not easy. One had to wait for those windows of opportunity to enter. Saying or doing the right thing at the right time takes a lot of paying attention to the slightest word or tone or movement. This allows some entry into Brent's realm. I suspect it was our effort to understand him that gave Brent faith that we were showing him respect. For Rex and myself we knew if we gave Bent respect he would give us some in return. This was a simple lesson we learned or better yet, a lesson Brent taught us. This was never learnt by those supporting him in Woodlands and by only a few at Glendale and sadly we were unable to pass these teachings on to the pink house staff.

It was not that Rex and I kept this a secret to ourselves. The other staff at the program soon picked up the techniques we used to interact with Brent. I even offered to give an in-service to the home staff on our strategies for supporting Brent. I said that I would do this for free as my prior experience of asking to be paid for my time could get in the way. It was still not accepted. I clearly remember the social worker's reply to my offer of help: "You're not qualified." I took that to mean that I did not have the appropriate letters behind my name. Clearly the tools they were given by someone with the proper qualifications were not working. This reminded me of a scene in a Monty Python movie where the doctors were in a delivery room full of big, expensive machines and the soon-to-be mother askes the doctors, "What should I do?" The doctor's reply was, "nothing dear, you're not qualified."

Now to give an indication of the effectiveness of the different approaches between the day support and the support Brent was receiving at the pink house, I got some numbers from a friend who worked in the ministry. Turns out, in a nine-month period, the home had 280 serious incident reports submitted to the ministry office. In that same period the day program had nine. It would seem to indicate that we knew something the pink house staff didn't. The idea of sharing these different approaches was not embraced by Brent's social worker.

Brent had been thought of as a monster and the-powers-that be fed that premise with all the schemes developed for staff protection. The-powers-that-be sometimes need to be confronted by the-powers-that-ought to be. Although I tried, it fell on deaf ears. Brent was clearly communicating that this residential set-up was not working for him and it evidently was not working for the staff. As he was attacking home staff way more than the staff at the day program then one would think that the more successful place should be explored for the reasons why. This consideration did not happen. Instead, more staff protective measures were put into place at his house.

In the pink house vehicle they installed a plexiglass partition between Brent and the driver. I was told that on the drive to the program there were few incidents. It was on his way back that his aggression occurred. On one drive home Brent had hit the glass so hard that it became disconnected from its mounts. This caused another protocol to come into play. They were to pull over and call the police. As the staff described to me, the constables showed up and asked few questions. They proceeded to drag Brent from the vehicle, put him face down in the gravel and handcuffed him. I was told that after these metal restraints to his wrists were in place, he was forcefully put into the backseat of the police car. Then they delivered him back to his house. Treated like a criminal when the real injustice was a lack of imagination from those who were responsible for making plans for his care.

The situation at the pink house grew worse. They kept doing what was not working. Sadly, the same "qualified" person who wrote behaviour support plans for Brent at Glendale was now advising the Pink house staff on the best way to help Brent in the community. It didn't work very well at Glendale and it was having the same results in his new home. Go figure.

EVACUATE... THAT'S THE TICKET

"...things are never as complicated as they seem. It is only our arrogance that prompts us to find unnecessarily complicated answers to simple problems."

Muhammand Yunus

I was again approached by this very attentive social worker and asked if we could provide day support seven days a week, as we were only a Monday-to-Friday operation. The weekends were not going well at the home so I took the 9 a.m. to 3 p.m. Saturday shift and Rex took the Sunday. It seemed that I was qualified to physically and emotionally care for Brent but to direct others in how to do this, well for that I needed to have had more education.

During this time Brent had hurt a few staff at the pink house. Brent's ability to put staff off on injury compensation continued. The person who wrote the behavioural support procedure was asked to help this "staff injury" problem. The plan devised was very successful and foolproof: It was called the "evacuation plan". Here's how it worked: Whenever Brent became agitated, the staff would evacuate to the other side of the house. They had closed-circuit cameras installed so that when Brent showed any signs of agitation, staff would leave, as per protocol, they could keep an eye on Brent via the TV. This worked great: they could watch Brent and not get hurt. It was foolproof: they couldn't get hurt by Brent if they were nowhere near him. Problem solved, for the staff. Brent's problem not solved. But the staff injury problem was well addressed.

I witnessed how this worked and what could trigger the evacuation procedure. One afternoon I had to return Brent to the pink house because their van was in the shop. One could enter Brent's side of the house but you could not get out without a key. Brent and I went in and the staff were not on his side. So while waiting for a staff to show up I wandered around. Brent had a particularly good day. He was in a great mood, so much so he asked me to get him a sheet from the locked cupboard. I told him, "No can do. No key." That was when a staff arrived. A very nice fellow, we said our hellos, I told him of Brent's good day and I asked for a key so I could get Brent a sheet. I told the staff how he had special sheets. No sooner did I say that when the house staff went to the locked door and told me we had to evacuate. I was confused; I saw no signs of agitation. I asked the staff what the deal was, Brent was not pissed off, in fact, he was very chipper. The house staff told me that, "if he asks for something he can't have then that leads to agitation." This request fell into the evacuation category. I suggest that this program focused the staff's attention towards all the signs written by the qualified person to bugger off. They were scared of him and even at the slightest tone change, or request that fell under the heading of agitation or anger, the staff would follow the plans to evacuate and their fears of injury would be gone. Brent was not a beneficiary of this clever plan. I said that Bent was smart but it would take a huge leap to think he could learn something from this action. Rather than teaching Brent that if he remained calm the staff would hang around, he just learned that, for no reason he could comprehend, these folks would just leave him alone. His home often became a big time out room, the only difference was the staff did not take him to the room, they just abandoned him there.

I noticed that when the staff decided he should leave, he gave no information to Brent as to why he was leaving. It was as if they thought Brent could not understand what they would say to him. I suggest that if they had given him credit for being smarter he would have caught on to the evacuation plan and it might have had an effect on how he behaved. A lack of understanding and a lack of respect of Brent was the main reason this plan was doomed to failure.

BIFF

"If you believe in a cause, be willing to stand up for that cause with a million people or by yourself."

Otis S. Johnson

I have an example of how, to the letter, this program was followed. Beth told me that she came to work at Brent's place on a Sunday at 2 p.m. She arrived at the pink house to find the two staff tasked with supporting Brent sitting at the kitchen table in front of the closed-circuit TV. Brent being the star of this show, alone in his side of the house. Beth said she could see Brent walking around in his place in pajamas and it was obvious to her that he had soiled and wet himself. Turns out he had a bit of diarrhea upon waking and I suspect he had cramps and thus was agitated. Boom, off the staff leave as per the plan. Beth, who had worked with Brent at Glendale, was a gal who was rough around the edges but a softie at heart. She told the staff that she was going in to clean up Brent. She was abruptly told by her co-workers that she could not do that because the protocol says they had to have two staff go in and neither of them were willing to go with her. The rules also stated that they could not go in until he had settled down. I am sure Beth said something along the lines of, the hell with that, or even stronger language. Off she went, policy procedure and plan be dammed. When she entered the room, Brent said "Biff" (Brent could not properly pronounce Beth's name) "Could you clean him up?" And that is just what she did.

Another thing about this evacuation plan: they had to lock the bathroom because they could not place a camera in there. Therefore, Brent could not accesses the bathroom during this evacuation procedure. This is a big problem if a guy had the trots: nowhere to go but in your strides.

With the bathroom door opened and a tub run, Beth set to clean up Brent. She said it took three times of soaking and rinsing to get him clean of the dried-on filth. She said the other staff did help after they saw that Brent had settled. Beth said that he was tired and the rest of her shift was mostly spent with her watching TV and having Brent's head on her lap.

The next day Beth came to work at 2:00 and was told she had to see the manager. In the office was the house manager's boss. This was a fair-sized organization with many homes. The manager's boss lit into Beth. He said she had violated protocol and if she had gotten hurt it would have been her fault and such. She was told that the rules were there for a reason and needed to be followed. For this act of insubordination she was sent home for one day without pay and upon her return she was told she could no longer work on Brent's side of the house as she was getting too close to him in a personal way.

Beth was a person who Brent trusted. She was not scared of him and she showed him respect. And now she was out of his world. Policy, paper and protocol before people: a sad way to prioritize care. I must note that this house manager was not the villain in this situation; she knew Beth had done the right thing for Brent. It was the manager's boss who took offence to Beth's actions. When the report of what happened on that Sunday got to the manager's boss's desk it was out of her hands. Again, the house had good people working there; the problem was they had to follow a poorly thought-out plan and I would also say an abusive one.

IT'S BACK TO WOODLANDS FOR YOU BRENT!

"My father used to say 'Don't raise your voice. Improve your argument."

Archbishop Desmond Tutu

As things got worse for Brent and the staff at the pink house the social worker decided, perhaps at the direction of qualified people, that the two-to-one staffing that Brent had should be bumped up to three to one. This drove up the costs of residential care for Brent to $430,000 a year, over four times the cost of a normal group-home placement. Sadly, doing more of what is not working has never been a good idea, from both humane and economic perspectives. It reminds me of the man who was heading into his fourth marriage, the thought being that hope had triumphed over experience.

Due to these costs something had to change. I am sure that is why I received a call from Brent's sister on a Sunday morning. She was very upset. She told me that Brent's brother was called to a meeting the previous Friday and at this meeting it was decided that Brent would be better cared for at the Willow Clinic in Vancouver. Brent's sister was out of town then so she could not make the meeting. I explained to Sherry that Willow Clinic was the cottage that was built on Woodlands grounds in the 1950s. At this meeting it was decided that Brent would be sent back to the Woodlands grounds- the same walls he was sent to when he was 9 years old. These grounds and buildings went from being an asylum, then a school and now a clinic with the hopes of taking the edge off what it really was. This was no walk in clinic, oh you could walk in but to get out one would need a key!

The original reason he was sent there was because his parents could not support him in their home. Now the reason was that the government and the ministry responsible could not find a way to support him in his community. I suggest that it was mostly driven by the inflated costs due to poor planning and the pig-headedness of doing more of what was not working and ignoring other ideas. They seemed to want to double down on dumb at Brent's expense.

Sherry, Brent's sister, was beside herself. She recalled what happened last time her brother went to Woodlands and she would not let it happen again. Sherry said to me, "you have to do something." I told her not to worry, I'd think of something. I told her to call the social worker and set up a meeting for mid-week. She told me, "They don't know who they are dealing with." I soon found out what she meant. She said she would get back to me as soon as she got a meeting set. She hung up and I had to think of something. I said I would but I did not have a clue of what I was going to do.

I had a meeting the next afternoon with a colleague, a woman who, like myself, presented at the community support-worker course at the local college; the same course I had taken in 1981. I told her the story of how the decision was made to send Brent back to Woodlands. Penny, a tiny woman with a huge presence, also a big supporter of community living and the rights of persons with developmental disabilities. She always carried herself with grace and dignity. She was smart quick-witted and took very seriously her role as an advocate for persons with developmental disabilities. I also thought she was very "proper" and would not say shit if she stepped in it. So after I told her the details of what was planned for Brent she said, "That's bullshit." Two things occurred to me at that moment: First, I was shocked that she would swear. Second, I was empowered to, "do something," as Sister Sherry had requested. To be honest I was scared of the ministry- a powerful organization and the funder of my society and the Namaste day program. They were a giant to take on and I feared for my job. It was Penny's words that made me realize that she, and others like her, would be in my corner and help when I needed it. With her support I was ready for the fight ahead.

Later that afternoon I called Sherry and told her we would not let this happen. I wrote a hastily prepared proposal where I would train staff and house Brent in a spare bedroom at the day program. After we had Brent dialed in or, better put, when Brent had dialed in the staff, I would then pass his care onto an agency that did this sort of thing, with the staff Brent and I had trained. It was only a temporary care plan; I had no desire to provide 24-hour care for the long term. I submitted this proposal to the ministry a few days before the scheduled meeting.

This was when I really got to know Brent's siblings. Turns out they were very much like him. They were not pushovers and a scrap did not scare them. Sherry, Bruce and I became very tight in our fight to keep Brent from going back to Woodlands.

The decision to send Brent back to Woodlands was made quickly and with little or no consultation with me or his family. When it was announced that the best place for Brent was that old institution, Bruce did not know how to react. It had been Sherry who attended most of these meetings. Bruce was told by those at the meeting that this was the best place for his brother and he felt they gave him no place to comment.

When Bruce called his sister, Sherry told me he said, "We can't let them do this again to our brother." She told me that was the first time Bruce had referred to Brent as "his brother." Bruce was 17 when Brent was born and was out of the house well before Brent was sent to Woodlands. With Brent's challenges his mother put all her attention toward him and this may have caused some resentment from Bruce.

Bruce obviously knew Brent was beat up in Woodlands when he was sent there last time. When the three of us met to go over strategy Bruce became the protective big brother.

I went over the proposal with them and we discussed how to react if the proposal was rejected. Sherry was also being a protective big sister and said, "If they don't agree to the proposal they better get ready to see me dancing on the tables," meaning she would kick up a fuss the likes they had never seen before.

PUSH BACK

"If you avoid conflict to keep peace, you start a war inside yourself."

Unknown

I quickly put together a proposal to support Brent residentially and hand delivered it to the district supervisor. We talked for a while then he said that my proposal will be reviewed and he would get back to me shortly. The following is the letter he sent me:

"Feb 18, 1997

Terry Flatt

C/o Namaste Society

Dear Terry:

Re: Brent Smith / Interim Residential Support Plan

I am writing in response to our February 17, 1997 meeting. I appreciate the commitment and advocacy you have demonstrated on behalf of Brent Smith but I am not able, at this time, to consider your residential support plan for him. Brent is one of the most challenging men in the province to support in a community based residential setting. While I acknowledge that you are intimately familiar with Brent and his needs you have not had any experience operating a 24 hour staffed residential facility.

Brent can be aggressive without antecedents and can potentially place both himself and his caregivers at risk. His behaviour at times demands a specialized intervention. With the support of Willow Clinic, his present home staff have used withdrawal from Brent's environment to ensure Brent's safety. Namaste has used physical restraint as a last resort to ensure Brent's safety. I know your program has attempted at all costs to avoid this intervention. In the absence of other options, caregivers are often forced to use physical restrain to protect others from harm. Any community based resource which is planned for Brent must be carefully developed over time with input from all stakeholders. Willow Clinic, in my opinion, provides the best interim option for Brent Smith.

Given the demands of managing Brent's complex behaviors, I support his admission to Willow Clinic at this point in time, pending the development of a permanent community based resource. I am not prepared to place you at risk as a contractor, or Brent as a resident.

The ministry is ultimately responsible for Brent's safety and well-being in any community based resource. You do not have direct experience in managing a specialized residential facility. There have been some administrative omissions with your current program. Critical incidents have not on occasion been submitted. This further raises my concerns regarding your ability to administer a residential program of this complexity at this juncture. You have also demonstrated an inability at times to maintain a sense of balance in a politically sensitive environment. I would not have difficulty with this if your only interest was advocacy for Brent. You have an interest in being a contractor, if only on an interim basis, and need to be scrupulous in your communication, and accurately aware of all dynamics which may be operation at any given time.

The Ministry is not prepared to take any risks with supporting Brent in the community. His best interest at this point in time would be best served by admission to Willow Clinic. I recognize you have a lot to contribute in the planning for Brent, and would encourage your further involvement. Your input and suggestions regarding residential planning are most welcome and encouraged. Thank you for your interest and advocacy to date on Brent's behalf."

The bottom of the letter had a list of others who would get this letter: the area manager, the advocate for service quality and others with big titles. I was pissed but I knew that anger needed to be kept in check. I knew that reacting negatively would not be helpful to Brent's situation. I did not need to give the ministry ammunition to say that I was emotionally unstable. I needed to react professionally if I wanted to save Brent from being taken away and placed on the same Woodlands grounds he went to 28 years prior.

MY REPLY:

"Failure is the opportunity to begin again more intelligently."

Henry Ford

I would like to respond to your letter to me dated February 18th re; Brent Smith / Interim Residential Support Plan. Please understand this letter is not disputing your decision to reject my hastily prepared proposal. I agree that you are ultimately responsible for Brent and I am confident the decision is based on your opinion of what is best for him. I do wish to make a comment, a clarification, an observation and a word of defence with certain matters of this letter.

I take exception to the labelling of Brent (in his present state) as, "one of the most challenging men in the province to support." Anyone who came in contact with Brent at our program the day you wrote the letter (and for the last four months) would not have described him that way. When labels are attached to others they should be based on what they are now and not what they were.

Regarding my lack of experience operating a 24 hour facility. In my proposal I also acknowledge this fact. It is due to this lack of experience that I proposed to have Lisa (house manager of a behavioral group home for the past five years) to fill that area of expertise that I do not have. I do understand the ministry's reason for not taking a risk on a "contractor" without a track record in this area.

Concerning Brent's aggressive behavior and the potential for harm to come to Brent or staff. Brent's aggressions have been virtually non-existent in the last four months while at the day program. When Brent is unhappy, he is more likely to become aggressive. For the last four months at the program he can best be described as happy. At this time the demands of "managing Brent's complex behavior" is not very complex when he is with the staff at Namaste. It stands to reason that the risk to Brent and staff is and would be small. I accept however that you are responsible for Brent's safety. We at Namaste, for the last year have been successfully responsible for Brent's safety. I am confident that if Brent goes to Willow Clinic they will also be successful in the area of safety.

I would like to defend myself against your accusation that I am famous for "administrative omissions." This slight oversight was dealt with in a letter to your office dated Nov. 12, 1996. It seems petty to bring up this small omission that has long since been rectified. I am also insulted at the implication that my advocacy for Brent may be tainted because I also want to be a contractor. I founded Namaste as a society because I believe people should not make a profit on providing human services. I am also on the board and vice-chair of Citizens Advocacy of Victoria. I have a strong sense of what friendship means to a person with a disability and when they need an advocate. I made it very clear at the meeting that the reason I put forward this proposal was as an option to his placement at Willow Clinic. This was done at Brent's sister's request and you should have no difficulty believing her motives. I am also sure that I would have been much more scrupulous in my communication if I was involved in all the dynamics of this situation. I was not invited to the Feb. 4, 1997 meeting when the decision was made to send Brent to Willow Clinic.

You can be sure that I will need no encouragement to be involved in further advocacy for Brent and his family.

I also sent this letter to all the folks the district supervisor's letter went to. It was the area manager, this social worker's direct supervisor that decided to give my proposal a look. She called for a meeting with the stakeholders rather than rubber stamp the complete rejection that was clear in the Feb 18th letter.

LONG HALLWAYS

"To see what is right and not do it is the worst cowardice."

Confucius

Attending the meeting were all the stakeholders: Brent's brother and sister, management of the organization presently providing care for Brent, two social workers, the regional manager who was the boss of those social workers, and me. The meeting started off with Brent's social worker, the person who signed off on the 3:1 staffing and the evacuation procedure. It was his recommendations that caused the huge costs to support Brent in the pink house. He was also the person who pooh-poohed my offer to help the house staff better understand Brent.

This social worker started off the meeting with a lecture on the cost to taxpayers to have Brent supported in the community. In human services, when "efficient action" is needed due to funding issues they are almost always unjust. I could tell he was pulling out all the stops to impress his boss: he wore a tie and adult shoes. After educating us on where the funds came from to support Brent, he moved on to the benefits of Brent heading back to the old Woodlands grounds. On a big white board he wrote down the word PROS and under that he wrote "Brent likes long hallways." He then explained that at Willow clinic, they had such hallways. I spoke up and asked for a CON list and then proceeded to rattle off the following: 1. Brent has established strong relationships with Rex, me and other day-program staff. 2. Brent's remaining family would require a six-hour round trip to see him. 3. Brent has plenty of places with long hallways that he can access in his community.4. Our day program can and does provide support for Brent without incidents of major aggression.

The PRO list looked a little sparse compared to what Brent would lose by leaving his community and the town that he was familiar with. There was much more I could have added but I felt that four to one was enough.

The proposal I submitted to provide residential care for Brent was more than half the cost of what was then being spent at the pink house as this support could be done with just one properly trained person. I was confident in my ability to do this as I was able to do it with the four other staff at the day program with relative ease.

During the meeting, the representative of the pink house spoke up. This person proceeded to detail how destructive Brent could be, and talked about doors being ripped off their hinges and the staff injury stuff. He built a horror floor of what damage Brent was capable of and almost everything he said was true: Brent had done all those things. What triggered these behaviours however went unexplored. The fact that he was not being listened to and that he seemed to be respected only because of his aggression and not his intellect was a shame. That being said, this agency was a fine organization and had done many good things for many persons with developmental disabilities who came out of Glendale, but due to poor planning and direction they missed the mark on supporting Brent.

Soon after the pros and cons were laid out, the regional boss of the ministry, who had read my proposal, asked if I would be willing to provide this residential support long term rather than just the four months written in the proposal. I remember looking down at my adult shoes (I wanted to make an impression as well) for a moment, thinking about making this commitment. This was a big deal for me. I then thought this was a bigger deal for Brent. If I said "no" he would likely be shipped off to Woodlands. I lifted my head and said, "If that is what it will take to keep Brent in his community, you bet." The boss lady said to her subordinates, "set it up." The meeting was over and Brent was staying. I had to get things in place and quickly as every night he spent at the pink house was hard on Brent and the staff supporting him.

DO SOMETHING... I SAID I WOULD

"Bravery is not the absence of fear. Bravery is feeling the fear, the doubt, the insecurity, and still deciding that something else is more important."

Mark Manson

As was noted in my letter I had my friend Lisa help with the paperwork. With her expertise we could properly set up the administrative logistics. Lisa also knew Brent from her time at Glendale. There was one day when Rex had pulled into her group-home drive way to deliver something. Lisa stuck her head in the window and said her hellos to Brent and then went on to talking to Rex. I guess she was going on too long for Brent's liking so he politely said, "Hey Lisa." She replied, "Yes dear." Brent then said, "Lisa, if I gave you two bucks would you shut the hell up?" Lisa smiled and replied, "Oh Brent, it would take much more than that." Rex says Brent was smiling the whole time.

The initial plan was to turn a bedroom at the day program, which was run out of a house, into a room for Brent so the housing cost to the ministry was zero. We would use the day program van so no real extra transportation outlay and the staffing expense would be two thirds less as my plan needed only one properly trained staff, rather than three poorly guided employees at the pink house. I thought the staffing budget would be way less until I met with the social workers who were given the orders to set it up. This meeting was the day after the go-ahead. At this meeting was the representative from the pink house and the two social workers. The main social worker started off by informing me that the one-to-one staffing ratio was not adequate and he demanded two-to-one staffing. Not wanting to argue, I agreed.

Next on the agenda was adding more costs- a destruction cost. The social worker said the ministry would provide an additional $500 a month in the budget for damages Brent surely would cause at the day-program facility. I thanked him for his generosity, but felt this would not be needed. Saying this was a mistake, as this set off the pink house agency representative. He went on a tangent about how we would need to put ¾-inch plywood on the walls as Brent would kick holes in the drywall and that I would need to get heavy outside doors to replace the inside doors as the inside doors were flimsy and Brent would rip the door handles right off. Oh, and everything will need to be screwed down as Brent would pick it up and use it as a weapon. I listened politely then told them, "We will not be replacing the doors." This set him off again. I explained that, with all due respect, it was when Brent was left alone during the evacuation plan that he did this destruction and when Brent got upset we would stay with him and help him through his issues as we had for the past 10 months at the day program. I also said, "Our support strategies will be and have been different than yours, and it has shown that the way we have provided support for Brent, he had not needed to communicate his frustrations with this type of behaviour." Anyway, the meeting ended and some feathers were ruffled but the $500 per month we didn't need stayed. So much for the concern for taxpayers' money.

Someone said: "No good deed goes unpunished," and I found this out when I went to meet about the wages for the one-too-many staff in Brent's new residential placement. I went in thinking I would be able to ask for more than the average support-worker hourly rate due to the almost half-a-million cost per year they were willing to spend with the pink house. I was wrong. I came in with a high number. The ministry representative counters with a low one. I lowered mine, and he came back with the same low offer. I said, "Come on, Dave, this is not how you play this game. I go down you come up, we meet in the middle." Dave was a nice man and he told me that is the best he could offer. If I wanted more I'd have to go above him. Then he told me about the last time he "went upstairs." His request for a new battery to power an electric wheelchair was declined. He was told that the organization needed to find the money from their budget. So with this in mind I conceded. I would take what they gave me. Brent did not have the luxury of time. Also I did not want to jeopardize the chance of the deal falling through over money.

I thought the deal was done and I could hunt for staff, knowing what the hourly wage would be. Dave said, "Not so fast." "There is one more thing that has to get cleared up." You see, there was a complaint filed regarding Brent going into my care. There was a letter, signed by some of the pink house staff as well as those working for the Community Crisis Team. They had grave concerns about Brent's safety with me. I was told this letter of complaint alleged that the reason Brent was so well-behaved with me and the day-program staff was because we must have been "man-handling" Brent, and he was better behaved with us due to Brent's fear of stepping out of line. Now, Brent was not afraid to step out of line when he was nine in Woodlands, where he was "man-handled." Nor was he afraid when he was tossed into time-out at Glendale. This was a strategy that never worked then, so why would we use it now? Not sure where they got this idea on how we successfully supported Brent.

I learned about the contents of this letter from Beth, who worked at the pink house and she was asked to sign it. She refused because she knew how I and the program staff supported Brent. She was one of the few who hung around at the program after she dropped off Brent. During this time she saw how we used humor and how we took the time to listen to Brent; we took time to wait for him to digest the options he was given and how we would work with him to help him through his inner frustrations. Turns out, as Beth told me, she was let go, or asked to leave the pink house because she would not sign that letter, something about not being a team player. When I found that out I hired her.

It was not long until a short investigation revealed Brent faced no imminent danger on my watch, so I was off to the races.

I'M NOT MAD YOU KNOW

"Being honest may not get you a lot of friends but it'll always get you the right ones."

John Lennon

I had four staff lined up and was given three days of funding for training. The training took less than three hours. The new staff were given simple rules to follow: respect Brent and don't be afraid of him. I did give some details of what this respect looked like:

1. Don't lie to him. If you say you will be doing something or give him something then you had better deliver. Don't think he will forget because he won't.
2. Understand that he is smart, smarter than his actions would indicate. Understand that if he does not answer your question right away, that does not mean he didn't hear you. He will answer if he thinks it is necessary or once he has thought about the answer.
3. Have a sense of humour. Have fun as that lets him know you are not afraid of him.

I told the new staff that Brent always has a reason for his aggression or agitation so don't give him a reason, showing fear or a lack of respect is reason enough.

Here is an example of Brent's ability to sense fear in others. Rex and I took Brent to the doctor as he needed to be checked out in order to get his teeth looked at by a dentist. You know blood pressure and such, to ensure that he could safely undergo the anesthetic.

The three of us entered the waiting room and Brent was full of beans, talking loudly, making little sense, so we were soon hustled off to an examination room where we waited a while. We had some fun with the rubber hammer testing his reflexes, he was in a great but loud mood. The door opened and the doctor's assistant comes in with a bathroom scale. She came in, and I would guess, feeling a bit scared. Brent reached out and grabbed her arm gently and she froze. Brent said in a very calm voice to her, "I'm not mad you know, I'm not mad." He could tell she was scared and he did not want her to be.

Another example of Brent's awareness was when we got the news they wanted to send Brent back to Woodlands. It was at the day program and it was after most of the other participants had left. Brent was wandering around the house with his keys, seemingly engrossed in opening and closing doors. While Brent was occupied, Rex and I were talking about the chance that Brent would be sent away and, if so, Rex would be out of a job. I reassured Rex that I was working on a plan to stop it. Rex then noticed Brent's shoe was untied. Rex got him to sit down so he could tend to this lace. I guess Bent sensed that something was amiss with Rex and he proceeded to pat him on the back and said, "Don't worry, Rexman, Flattie will fix it."

Brent's observation skills are also acute. Joe, a staff with the day-program, was a big guy with a similar sized appetite. His lunch preparation was a production indeed. So one Saturday when it was just Brent and me he opened the fridge and started to haul out the contents. He then placed them neatly on the counter. I was allowing Brent new freedoms and I just let him do it. I waited till he had emptied the ice box, then I asked him what he was doing. He looked at me and smiled, "that's how Joe does it."

Giving Brent freedoms would have been new to him. He was allowed to do only what others wanted. I decided to let him do just about anything he wanted, as long as he asked nicely and was not hitting anyone. We needed to give him a replacement for his aggression. He soon realized that he could get more if he used politeness, kindness and his abundant charm. Three things that he had plenty of but these characteristics were nowhere to be found in any written information regarding him.

I told the new staff many of the positive things about Brent. The stories of how smart he was, how funny and affectionate he could be. I gave them the history from Woodlands to Glendale and the pink house experience. I painted a three-dimensional human picture of him and, when describing his massive reputation, I kept going back to him being misunderstood by those wanting to provide support. I told these new staff that this misunderstanding stopped here and with them.

I had one more meeting with the social worker at the ministry just before he moved out of the Pink house. I was told that Brent was deemed, "the second-most difficult person in the province to provide care in the community" I thought to myself, "Damn, it Brent, if you had tried harder you could have been number one!" The other thing I found interesting was he said "You have caused a big change in Brent." I was quick to correct him. I said, "If you put Brent back into that same type of environment that misunderstood him and had people around him that were scared of him, he would be busting heads again." I went on to say that it was not me that changed him because he has not changed. His environment changed. Those who supported him had a different attitude and understanding of him. When we stopped looking at him as a monster he stopped being one.

Training done and staff in place, I went on a Sunday morning to pick up Brent from the pink house. So with his few possessions we were off. There were no tearful goodbyes and he seemed to understand that he would never have to go back.

We drove to the day-program facility were his new living situation would be. I told the new staff that Brent likes nicknames so it was decided that the two guys would be called Skipper Dave and Captain Mike. Brent was clearly happy on the drive, yapping away and after I told him about the names of the guys he was going to meet he had already shortened the names to Skip and Cap. We arrive, and the connection with the guys was instant. They knew what to do and what not to do. Coffee was made and Brent's yammering went on. He had sized up the new staff and he seemed to approve.

The guys went home after we had dinner and it was just Brent and me. We had yet to get another staff on board. (Beth was recovering from an operation). But there were other trained staff ready to step in. It was my hope that with all the excitement of the move, Brent would be tired and would want to go to bed early. This was not the case. I was beat and ready for a rest. His room was set up and he had a nice long soak in the tub. A cup of decaffeinated coffee and off to hit the sack. I had set up a cot just outside his room in order to be close by if he needed to use the toilet in this new living arrangement. Brent was tucked in and I turned off the light, but that didn't turn off his mouth. He was real chatty, flapping his gums about Cap and Skip, with a few Rexmans thrown in. I would be just nodding off then he would yell, "Flattie," then inform me about his new friends and such. I firmly said to him "Shut up and go to sleep." I was surprised; there was silence for a few minutes then he yells, "I love you Flattie" I yelled back, "I love you too. Now shut up." And he did.

DIDN'T KNOW HE COULD BE AROUND PEOPLE:

"Everything we hear is an opinion, not a fact. Everything we see is a perspective, not truth."

Marcus Aurelius

Brent was doing well in our care at the day-program house, but the social worker who made the case to send him back to Woodlands seemed to have his doubts regarding our ability to successfully provide support for Brent. We had way too many meetings for my liking. One meeting in particular was regarding the crisis team, and what their role would be in this new arrangement. When we all sat down, I was quick to explain that we did not need this kind of crisis service. This seemed to be what this social worker was waiting for, an opportunity to direct me on what Brent needs. After a long-winded big-worded rant he said I was, alienating Brent from community supports, this sent me into my own rant, perhaps not as long-winded and certainly with fewer big words. I pontificated (a big word) that it was with these types of supports that Brent was abandoned in his own home. It was with these supports that Brent was agitated, aggressive and hurting staff. I absolutely agreed that I was alienating him from these supports because they seemed to be of little or no use to Brent. If they did, he would still be living at the Pink house. I went on to explain that we now had people who knew Brent and they would come to his aid in times of need, rather than having strangers with zero experience with him and with no relationship and no understanding of what they needed to do to help him.

This rant of mine didn't go over very well and I was soon summoned to a meeting with this social worker's new boss. I was told I would meet with the crisis team and I would fill them in on how we would use their help. So a time was set up for the crisis team to come to the program to discuss the strategy that they would use when they would inevitably be called.

The crisis team arrived for a meeting soon after the day program participants had left. Brent was sitting at the table having a coffee with Mick sitting right beside him. The two fellows on the crisis team seemed shocked to see this. One guy said, "I didn't know he could be around people." Like so many others in the community-support system that I was alienating Brent from, only saw him as one-dimensional and could therefore only relate to him that way.

Brent stopped hitting others but in times of internal frustrations he will hit himself. He will have loud conversations with himself, "That's it, no more of that," "I've had it with you, do you want another," "Have you learnt your lesson," followed by a hard slap to his face or a bite to his arm. These conversations seem to be a form of reverting to his institutional days, re-living the physical and verbal abuse he endured. It seems like he is playing both roles, the abuser and the one being abused. We support him through these times by becoming part of the conversation. We jump in to defend him, we say "Be nice to him, Brent's a good man." We use Brent in the third person as he does. We try to be the defender that was absent during his days in Woodlands.

Brent indeed could be around people but they had to be the right people.

HE NEEDS TO KNOW WHO'S IN CHARGE!

"You can't manipulate people who know how to think for themselves."

Trish Mercer

Seeing as we were going to receive a crazy man, we were ordered by Brent's social worker that all who would be supporting him would take some training on how to defend themselves, as well as how to restrain a person- that person being Brent. It seemed odd to me that during the 10 months Brent was coming to day program, this type of training was not imposed but now that he was going to be supported residentially this training was mandatory.

The person doing the training was Larry, the head hands-on crisis team person. Now I should give you what I understood this team to be. They sat at the Bat Cave, an emergency respite house, and if there was a behaviour emergency, they were called. Pretty sure it was by phone and not a spotlight in the night sky. I always wondered what the mayor of Gotham City would do to get hold of Batman and his sidekick Robin if they were needed during the day. I digress. Anyway, I think there were always two people ready to come to the rescue at any time. Brent, I was told, was one of their best clients. I do believe they were often very welcomed by the staff of other homes who were in a situation where these extra bodies, with their skill set were helpful. In Brent's case their ability to help was nil.

I would like to pass on Herb Lovett's thoughts on the value of learning restraint techniques: *"Unfortunately, much more energy has gone into controlling violence than has been spent asking why anyone, regardless of label, would resort to physical aggression. Some service organizations pride themselves on the comprehensive training they provide to new employees on how to handle physical assault. These techniques have many names, although they all train the same thing: ways to restrain people from doing something or ways of forcing people to move from one place to another. All of these techniques assume that, sooner or later, we need to know how to respond to violence from people we serve. Agencies that routinely train staff in these techniques generally do not spend comparable time considering how the restrained person finds this behavior adaptive. People in direct service who have been trained to wrestle clients to the floor when they do not do what staff want often have difficulty in seeing such extreme measures as cruel and unusual: "Walter has to learn he can't just do whatever he wants in life. I can't. Why should he?" "He needs to learn we're in control." The use of physical restraint reflects a passive acceptance of institutional history." People with psychoses* (which Brent has been diagnosed with having) *can be extremely challenging, but physical restraint is usually unnecessary except among strangers. As people labelled, moved out of these institutions, the habit of using restrains too often moved along with them, but restraining people only reinforces for everyone the stereotype that they are beyond reason and cannot control themselves. However, such institutional habits can be changed."*

Now during this training, Larry needed a volunteer to be the one restrained. Rick volunteered. Rick was a young strong man. He was only a few years away from playing hockey at a high level. Larry and his assistant got Rick in a hold that was said to be one that would render him unable to escape. Rick, with what seemed like very little effort, just stood up and was able to free himself. Larry was a bit sheepish seeing as he had guaranteed that using this restraint would be foolproof.

It should be noted that he crisis team were never called as they would have been way down the list of who would be summoned in case of an emergency. There would be no strangers coming to make Brent behave. It should also be noted that there was never a need for staff to restrain Brent in the manner we were shown after he moved from the pink house. A hug is used to stop him from slapping himself due to his frustrations and an embrace was not a tactic that this restraint expert taught us.

YOU HAVE TO BE CONSISTENT

"Arrogance is thinking you are above someone else, confidence is knowing no one is above you."

Habeeb Akande

The interference continued from the outside. There was a monitoring team that worked for the ministry, and they would come to go over the books as well as the behaviour programs that were set up. We were flagged for review from this team due to us supporting Brent. They seemed to come in looking for things that needed changing.

One of the things that we were directed to address was the many different written behaviour programs for dealing with Brent's agitation. They informed us that we could only have one program to follow. When I asked why, they said, "We had to be consistent." I had to explain that the way we supported Brent was based on creating a bond with him. I went on to explain that we are all different and therefore the rapport one person had with Brent was different than others that support him. We don't all possess the same personality traits or have the same tools or skills. We had a few different support plans and the staff could choose the one that worked for them and Brent at that time. When a support plan demands everyone be robotic in their actions and reactions then a relationship- real, reciprocal and equitable relationship cannot be created. The only person who is consistent is dead, he or she are consistently dead. Being treated the same way by all who are in your life would be boring. What this team wanted Brent's support group to do would have not allowed them to build a connection with him. There would be no growth or change. The things that we all were consistent with was listening to him, respecting him and not being afraid of him. We kept the multiple support programs. Again, people coming into Brent's world, with no idea of who he was and what he needed to cope in life and giving direction that would have led him right back to the location he had just come from…a controlling, robotic and relationship void environment. I held my tongue but wanted to shout at them and the other meddling people "You have no idea where you are going so get out of the way!"

YOU DON'T BELONG HERE.

"Without a sense of caring, there can be no sense of community."

Anthony J. D'Angelo

Brent did well at the day-program house but a real home was needed. This was a bit of an adventure because the "community" is not always a welcoming place for people thought to be different. I was able to find a place to lease-to-own, and it was a 10 minute walk from my house. When word got out, and it does fast in a small community, trouble started. The N.I.M.B.Y. (not in my back yard) was alive and well in my back yard. The following is the editorial in the local community newspaper.

"DISCRIMINATION, Esquimalt-style

Saxe Point neighbors should reconsider their opposition to group home. Esquimalt's Saxe Point transformed "neighborhood" into an ugly word last week.

Residents of the "exclusive" area managed to block the Namaste Transition to Employment Society from establishing a group home for three mentally handicapped men in a Munro Street house.

All the Society wants is to provide a home for the three men who would be under 24-hour supervision.

One of the residents who laboured mightily to block the group home is Esquimalt Coun. Jim King. He declared that group homes don't belong in "exclusive" neighborhoods.

Perhaps King should explain to his constituents exactly where in Esquimalt group homes do belong. "We support handicapped people," Insisted Murray Elphick, another Munro Street homeowner who worked to exclude the group home. "We just want to keep (Saxe Point) as a single-family zone here."

Elphick maintains that the men who would have been housed in the Munro Street group home wouldn't be a true family, and that a group home, even operated by a non-profit, is a business.

Legally, Elphick's argument is full of holes: under Esquimalt's regulations, up to four non-related adults can live in a house in neighborhoods zoned for single-family homes; under provincial law it's illegal to discriminate against people in group homes, and up to six clients are allowed to live in a licensed group home.

Morally, Saxe Points' rejection of the group home is appalling.

"There is deep-seated bigotry against handicapped adults" said Esquimalt Coun. Maurine Karagianis, the only person interviewed on the issue who wasn't afraid to call the opposition to the group home what it is. But then, as a mother of a son born with a physical disability, she recognizes discrimination when she encounters it.

Namaste executive director Terry Flatt was originally delighted when the lease-to-own arrangement was first made with the owner of the Munro Street property. But, "the bottom line is we were unable to move into the neighborhood because of the pressure," he said.

It is a shame the society didn't hang on a bit longer to see if there were some enlightened Saxe Point residents who would see nothing wrong with the group home and who would lobby to reverse their neighbors' minds. As it is, the whole neighborhood must share the same ugly image."

This article was followed up with one from the Victoria Times Colonist, June 18,[Th,] 1997.

"PROTESTS SCUTTLE GROUP HOME FOR HANDICAPPED

Councillor accuses some Saxe Point residents of bigotry

By Richard Watts

Bigotry-it's an ugly word.

But one Esquimalt councillor says it's the main reason why some residents of upscale Saxe Point rallied last week to chase a group home for mentally handicapped people out of their neighborhood.

"There is a deep-seated bigotry against handicapped adults" said Esquimalt Coun. Maurine Karagianis. As the mother of a son born with a physical handicap Karagianis is sensitive to bigotry. But she said even she was surprised at the intolerance she found over the Saxe Point incident.

The situation started when the non-profit Namaste Transition to Employment Society, which helps handicapped adults with housing, found a six bedroom house on Munro Street for sale.

Owner Bill Lang, a businessman who owns the Princess Mary restaurant, was asking $295,000. Lang said it soon became evident the neighbors were angry. "You could sort of feel it."

Meanwhile, Namaste was delighted with the deal destined to provide a home for three mentally handicapped men (Note: It was only Brent that was proposed to move in this home.) *who would be under 24-hour supervision. Terry Flatt, Namaste executive director, said government cutbacks mean there is no money for the province to buy houses for group homes. Lease-to- own arrangements, however, are perfect, he said. There is no need for a big down payment and tenants have security because the landlord can't cancel their lease on a whim.*

But by last week, with residents threatening petitions and Esquimalt Coun. Jim King openly vowing to stop the group home, Namaste backed out. "The bottom line is we were unable to move in because of the pressure" Flatt said.

Murry Elphick, a Munro Street resident who worked to keep the group home out said his opposition had nothing to do with the residents being mentally handicapped. But Elphick said a group home does not belong in his neighbourhood.

Besides not being a true family, a group home-even run by a non-profit group like Namaste-is a business, which is not allowed in a neighborhood zoned for single families, he said.

"We support handicapped people. We just want to keep (Saxe Point) retained as a single-family zone here"

King insisted he too, had nothing against group homes or mentally handicapped people. A group home does not belong in an upscale neighborhood he said.

King lives in the neighborhood.

He asked Karagianis to negotiate an agreement with Namaste to move into another house.

Officially, King was powerless to stop Namaste. Under Esquimalt regulations, up to four people who are not related can occupy a dwelling which is zoned for single families. Provincial laws which make it illegal to discriminate against people living in a group home, allow up to six clients in a licensed group home.

There was another small bit of reporting in the same Times Colonist paper:

"RESIDENTIAL GROUP HOME CONCEPT DEFENDED

A group home for people with mental handicaps can be the best neighbor in the world, say proponents.

Terry Flatt, executive director for Namaste Transition to Employment Society, said residents either have jobs or volunteer work to attend every day. Residents are driven by a staff member so cars don't line the street. They don't fix cars on the front lawn. They don't throw loud parties and they are usually in bed by 9 p.m. "they are Ozzi and Harriet neighbors," said Flatt.

And the people who live near a Namaste group home on Landsend Road in North Saanich back Flatt up. (Note: this home was not a Namaste group home. It was a home operated by another agency and those living there attended the Namaste day-program.)

"I can't see anything wrong with them in the neighborhood," said nearby homeowner Terry Anderson. "There have been no problems at all that I can think of."

Lesley Foster, who has two children, said she rarely noticed the residents of the Namaste home, except for the early evenings when they go for a walk.

"They are wonderful people. There is absolutely no problem at all."

Grant Hamer 17, a recent high school graduate, said he barely notices the Namaste home and can recall only one unusual incident. A resident had wandered off and Hamer's father helped with the search. "That is what good neighbors do for each other," said Flatt."

I attended a meeting with these concerned citizens. One person attending actually said, "I deserve to live in a neighborhood with people like me." I didn't say it but I thought about saying, "Oh, so you want to be surrounded by bigots huh." I thought about what would happen if that man had an accident and ended up with a disability that made him different. Would he be okay with people complaining about his wheelchair ramp and since, he was no longer like the rest of his neighbors, should move?

A LANDING FOR BRENT AND IT IS NOT WOODLANDS

"When a plant doesn't thrive, it may be in the wrong location"

Julie Flatt, Horticulturist

While this hub-bub was going on another lease-to-own situation came up and it was decided that although this was a fight we surely would win and, I was not afraid of the scrap, I however had the opportunity to avoid it. I had a realtor friend and he set things up for us with a lease-to-own with a big house on a huge lot. This was a house he had listed and by setting up this lease-to-own for us, he screwed himself out of a commission. Marcel was a good man indeed.

Another person who turned out to be a good man was Brent's meddling social worker. He was like the many others who had a big misunderstanding regarding who Brent was. He now saw that Brent was not a monster or a staff-hurting machine and if given the right environment he could thrive. Oh, he continued to stick his nose in where it didn't belong. An example was when I decided to call Brent's home, "The Goose House." The homes in the community are normally called the name of the street or road they were on. Brent's new home was on a street that is woman's name so I didn't think that would fit, but the property backed onto a regional bike trail and walking path called "The Galloping Goose Trail," so Goose House it was. This social worker protested saying it would send out the wrong message. Why not use the street name? I guess he thought if we named it the Goose House, then people would think that it was a home where people had their bums grabbed. Anyway, he turned the corner and was helpful in making this home happen.

I remember having lunch with this social worker and he told me he did what he thought was right at the time. I told him he just got bad advice from a person who had the primitive idea, to treat Brent's behaviour as if it were a symptom and it could be made to disappear with proper management. Brent just needed to be treated properly to begin with; then he would have no need for this behaviour. If he was fighting for respect and you give him respect then the fight is over.

So now Brent was rattling around this big house with one-too-many staff. We were approached by the ministry to support a man whose home-share situation was falling apart. He was also kicked out of his day program due to his newfound aggression and we at Namaste supported him during the day. We agreed to support him residentially with Brent. We had the staffing so why not. Things worked out for a while but Craig appeared to become jealous of Brent and the attention he received from the staff. This seemed to cause him to strike out at Brent. When staff would intervene, Craig would strike out at staff and have to be restrained. Brent oddly enough never retaliated against Craig's assaults. There was one time when staff were restraining Craig, Brent came up to him and said, "You got to understand, no Wrestlemania." My opinion of this verbal exchange was Brent trying to help Craig out by telling him the rules: don't hit and things will be great for you. Things eventually worked out for Craig. Rex decided that he would provide home support for him at his house and things went swimmingly for both of them. Craig became a member of Rex's home and all was well.

BRENT BECOMES FAMOUS AND I AM IN TROUBLE

"If you think you are too small to make a difference, you haven't spent the night with a mosquito."

African Proverb

While Brent was living at his new Goose house there was an article in the Times Colonist on November "11th, 2001.

MINISTER'S TARGET SHAMEFUL

A closer look

Jody Paterson

I can only take it as a battle cry, this indictment that cabinet minister Gordon Hogg has hurled at the province's disabled. More than $430,000 to care for a single person, exclaimed Hogg at last week's public cabinet meeting. Intolerable!

There is such a man in the Victoria area. He didn't however, come from the forensic Psychiatric Institute, as Hogg said.

He has come first from Woodlands and then Glendale, both of them institutions for the mentally handicapped phased out in B.C. over the last two decades.

Nor are there 200 such people costing us more than $400 a day for them, which Hogg also asserted at the meeting. There are in fact just 30.

The man singled out by Hogg is both mentally handicapped and mentally ill, with complex array of physical and behavioural problems.

He doesn't do well with other people and so he lives alone, or as alone as you can be with two round-the-clock support workers and another complex personality in the other suite next door.

His care and program costs total $49 an hour, which is not surprising given that it takes two people and they are unionized to provide it. Anyone who needed that much support would cost the same.

Providing care for people is an expensive business. We pay $125,000 a year to keep our aged citizens in a typical extended-care hospital in the capital region. We pay $61,000 a year to keep the criminal element in penitentiaries. I once knew a man waiting for a heart transplant who cost $550,000 in less than a year. But Hogg has set the limit at $430,000. Now we know: that's too much.

Implied in his statement is that the issue is not so much about caring for people as it is about drawing the line. His message is clear: If people with mental handicaps don't want to end up back at institutions, they'd better keep costs down.

It's not a threat that you can get away with for other groups, but this particular population hasn't yet been granted full peoplehood. They're low-status as is evident by Hogg's attack. I'd love to see the fallout if a cabinet minister were to call out an ailing elderly person and publicly condemn how much it costs to keep them in hospital.

Not that Hogg's comments were the first sign of a war. His ministry and the advocates for people with developmental disabilities have been lobbing ever–so-polite warning shots across each other's bow for months.

In an October discussion paper that sets the tone for major change and cutbacks, the Children and Family Development Ministry called for the contributions of other sectors of society, including families, individuals and corporations – weasel speak for dumping more costs onto families and non-profits that are already in desperate straits.

The B.C. Association for Community Living, an advocacy group for the mentally handicapped tersely responded by suggesting the ministry instead, "end bureaucratic restructuring that has drained resources from individuals and families."

We spend $526 million to support 8,700 people with developmental disabilities with two-thirds of that going to house 5,400 of them.

That is a fraction of the roughly 18,000 people with such disabilities on their own or living with families.

Hogg, making a giant assumption that larger groupings are cheaper to maintain, wants the ones in government care to live in groups of eight, maybe even 16, rather than four to six as is the case now.

To the disabled community, it all sounds just a little too much like the road back to where they came from, back into institutions.

A 16- person household is no longer a home. True, it's not yet 1,500 shuffling residents, isolation rooms, lineups 20 deep of naked people waiting to shower, teeth pulled out to stop "biters": all routine occurrences at B.C. three defunct institutions in their heyday. But for those who remember those days all too well, any step in that direction is alarming.

The government tells us we need to cut costs, and I am willing to accept that. But a civilized society spreads the pain around rather than singles out for special misery the population that are least able to protest.

Minimum-wage earners, hungry children, troubled teens, people on welfare, and now those with developmental disabilities...what a shameful list of sacrificial lambs this government has put forward in the name of getting its financial house in order. Is this how we'll pull ourselves toward economic recovery?

Think again, Gordon Hogg. Until you're ready to cap the price of care for every citizen, don't go picking on the handicapped ones."

So after reading this article I contacted my mole in the ministry, someone I knew there and trusted, to ask about this person in Paterson's article. Since the person spent time in Glendale perhaps I knew him and I could help out, the way I did with Brent. She told me that this story was about Brent. He was the guy who was costing $430,000 a year to support residentially in his community, and he was the person Hogg was talking about!

I thought it was a good idea to contact the reporter who wrote the story and have her meet the man cabinet minister Hogg was talking about. Here is Paterson's report on what she found:

"SMILES BELIE SCARY IMAGE OF The $430,000 Man

The $430,000 Man is behind me in the back seat, bugging the driver to turn up the radio. And I have to say, he's a bit of a disappointment.

I mean, the way cabinet minister Gordon Hogg made him sound, I thought he'd be scary. Uncontrollable. Dangerous. This guy is grumbling ever so quietly about a lack of coffee and wondering when he can listen to his George Thorogood tapes.

"For many who have been deinstitutionalized, it has been wonderful and they have blossomed," Hogg said a couple of weeks ago when he was complaining about having to spend $430,000 a year to house the mentally handicapped man. "I'm not sure that is true for someone like this person."

Hogg got it wrong. Brent Smith's life was much worse in the days when he was locked up in institutions, as was that of many of the staff who had to work with him. They frequently ended up injured when he went into one of his rages. He seemed particularly riled by blond women, and anyone in white clothes.

For a couple of years after he came out of Glendale in 1995, he was so aggressive that he needed three full-time workers assigned to him. That was the period when he cost the system $430,000 a year, a detail Hogg's speech writers apparently forgot to note.

These days, Smith has one worker and his care costs $276,000 with another $30,000 spent on day programs. These days, he's got nothing but smiles for blondes, including his pal who works at the Esquimalt gas station where he regularly goes for coffee.

"Hi cutie!" Candice Heinekey called to him after we pulled into the station Friday, reaching out to stroke his cheek. She says he stole a kiss from her last week.

Smith, 42, suffered massive convulsions three days after he was born. He never recovered from the brain damage. He was nine when his exhausted family realized they could no longer cope with him. They put him in New Westminster's Woodlands Institution, and then in Glendale when the facility opened in 1971.

He remained institutionalized long after most of the province's mentally handicapped had been moved to group homes. But eventually the last of Glendale's residents were relocated to. Smith among them.

His first residential placement was a disaster. The nervous family hired to care for him fled "if Brent so much as lifted a finger," recalls his sister Sherry Heisterman, and would watch him warily through a window until a crisis-response team arrived.

The four-person group home he moved into after that didn't work out much better. Then, as now, the government pressured Smith's family to re-institutionalize him in Willows clinic, the renamed remnants of Woodlands.

Heisterman made a desperate call to Namaste Society, which runs day programs for people with mental handicaps.

The Society put up Smith temporarily in its basement suite, then set up a house for him off the Galloping Goose Trail.

For the past four years, Smith has lived in the house with his worker. Heisterman says if a good match was found there's no reason a second person couldn't be moved in to the extra bedroom to cut costs.

The placement has left Smith a changed man. He's sociable and humorous, and rarely angry any more. Namaste executive director Terry Flatt knows why: Smith is simply grateful to finally regain some control over his life.

"He's a tough guy," says Flatt. "He fought, literally, to get where he is now, out from under the control of people in the institutions. If people get what they need, their negative behaviour goes away."

The one thing Smith wanted more than anything when Flatt first met him was a set of keys.

Flatt figures it's from the time in the institutions, when keys were what separated the staff from the residents, the powerful from the powerless.

Smith has his own set now, and he never lets them out of his sight. No sense in taking chances with freedom."

I was pleased with the story, the government was not. I got a call from someone high up in the ministry telling me that I was in big trouble,

I was in breach of my contract and that I was also in breach of confidentiality in putting Brent's name in the public realm.

Well I thought to myself, "Oh Magoo you really did it this time." I did what any coward would do, I called my friend Penny and said "help." She helped. The following is the letter she suggested I send in response to the claims of breach of contract and confidentiality:

November 20, 2001

To, [name redacted]

Services for Community Living

Dear [name redacted]

Further to our telephone conversation of Nov. 18, 2001, I am writing in response to your comments and your request that I describe and explain my involvement in the column written by Jodi Paterson, Times Colonist reporter.

First and foremost, I would like to express my very great concern at your statements that my involvement in this situation violates Namaste's contract with the ministry. I have been a contractor with the ministry for many years and my agency has a positive record of providing excellent services and advocating for community inclusion and community living for people in the Capital Region. Your charge is a very serious one, which is potentially damaging to our agency and its clients. If you still are of this opinion after reading this letter I request that you please specify in writing at your earliest convenience the terms of the contract which you believe have been violated.

As you know, the Times Colonist recently published a story about cabinet minister Gordon Hogg's comments in an open cabinet meeting in which he singled out an individual with challenging behaviour living in the Capital Region as an example of the high cost of community living services. Mr. Hogg also suggested that deinstitutionalization was not a success for such a person and that a congregate living arrangement might be more appropriate.

Reporter Jody Paterson later wrote an article questioning Mr. Hogg's comments and statements about community living services. I contacted Ms. Paterson to offer the perspective that community living has indeed been a success for individuals with challenging behaviour and that congregate care was not the answer for such individuals. Making such comments in public, when appropriate, is clearly within my agency's role in advocating for community living.

I told Ms. Paterson about the quality of life enjoyed by an individual, who once had very challenging behaviour, who is currently supported by our agency. Ms. Paterson expressed an interest in meeting this individual. With the individuals' sister's consent, I arranged for Ms. Paterson to meet this person and spend some time with him in the community. The result of this meeting was a very positive story about the success of community living for a person once thought to be unable to live successfully in the community.

To clarify several key points:

- *I did not identify this individual as being the individual discussed by Mr. Hogg.*
- *I did not authorize Ms. Paterson to identify this individual by name. I advised her that I did not have the authority to give consent for this.*
- *I answered Ms. Paterson's questions about the costs of this person's living arrangement, but as indicated, I did so with the belief that this would be presented as an anonymous example (as done by Mr. Hogg) and not identified as costs for a person named in this story.*

I know that we both share a commitment to community living for individuals with developmental disabilities. By working in partnership with the ministry, my agency has been able to meet the needs of very challenging individuals. My involvement in this story was an effort to share the results of this partnership and to provide a balanced and positive perspective on community living, and on the quality of life enjoyed by people who are receiving adequate supports in our community.

Regards,

Terry Flatt"

I did not hear back from the ministry. It was as if nothing had happened. The phone conversation was full of grave concerns but after this letter, the article and my indiscretions regarding it were never brought up again. It was not long before Brent received a hand-written Christmas card from Gordon Hogg that said the following:

"Nov 22/2001

Brent

I understand that your life may have been disrupted by a reference which I made to the range of cost for services which our ministry provides.

I apologized for any inconvenience which this may have caused you and I want you to know that my intent was not to identify anyone or define anyone in terms of money.

I understand that things are going well for you and I bestow my congratulations and best wishes for you and your family. Yours, Gordon Hogg"

HOW TO FIGHT A GIANT

"If you are afraid to defend your convictions because you might get your ass kicked for it, you are not really fit to advocate for them."

James Carlos Blake

I have had many other dealings with the decision makers and funders. The thing that advocating for Brent taught me was not to be intimidated with their perceived power. Being on the side of right does not sway them when making decisions that run contrary to the good of the individual. They sometimes feel they can say, "That's our decision," like they did with Brent and expect that to be the end of the discussion. We as advocates don't have to buy that nonsense. I almost fell for it with Brent. I thought them too powerful to fight. Obviously I was wrong. One does not have to accept an incorrect or misguided decision. One must fight, but one needs tips or tools for this fight. Word got out regarding my abilities to convince the power folks to re-think matters for the benefit of the individuals who need support. I have since been asked to help by a few parents to navigate the jungle of the system.

Most importantly is get things in writing. There are times that these folks will walk north and talk south. "Oh yes everything we do is in the best interest of the client." Unless it costs too much money then their actions do not match up with their words. Don't take their word for it. Write things down at meetings. Repeat what they have said. Ask "Are you saying that you agree that Bill should be approved for funding for three extra hours of recreational support?" Then ask when that funding can be expected.

When going to a meeting to advocate for an individual, have your points, concerns and wanted outcomes in writing. I have had them listen and verbally agree, with me and then they say later, "I don't recall you saying that at the last meeting." Having this happen to me in the past I now will come to meetings with what I wanted to say on paper. I read from it, then pass a copy to all attending so they cannot say they did not hear me say it.

MAKE THEM AN OFFER THEY CAN'T REFUSE

"To convince people don't try to reach their head, try to reach their heart."

Amit Kalantri

A father come to me for advice regarding his daughter who had just left high school and had entered the adult support services. She was autistic and had some behavioural issues. When frustrated she could become aggressive. This father described what the funders wanted to do for his daughter. They had a paid-for spot in a day program and she would be well supported there. This was not the case. She was bored. It was not a good fit for her. It was a good fit for the funders as it cost them no extra money for this placement. She was smart and wanted to do things with her time that interested her. Her dad told me that she would come home from this ill -suited program in a foul mood. This led to frustration, then to aggression towards her mother. This cheap and convenient placement for the funder was not working for this young woman. The father was basically told take it or leave it. He told me that if she continued to be aggressive towards her mother, their daughter would have to find a new place to live.

I asked him what type of day support, he thought would work best for his daughter. His eyes lit up as he described his vision for her. She was very smart and had a map of the city in her head. Her sense of direction was exceptional and she loved traveling around the city. Her father was in a business where documents needed to be moved about for signatures and such. He had pitched the idea to the funders that she would do well in a delivery or courier situation. His daughter would be the one who would, after finding out where things were to be delivered, decide on the most efficient routes to make the needed drop-offs and pickups that day. The father said that he would pay for the vehicle and all he needed was the wages for the driver covered by the funders. They refused this idea.

I came up with a plan to change their minds. I said, "You will make them an offer that they can't refuse." I wrote him a letter to read at the next meeting. I told him that when it was his time to speak that he should stand up to read it. He was a big guy and I suggested that they were trying to intimidate him; and now it was his turn to give it back to them. The letter went something like this: "The placement you want for my daughter is inappropriate for her. You are attempting to pound a square peg into a round hole. This causes her stress and frustration. This leads to aggressive outbursts at home. It is because of this misplacement I predict that she will hit my wife again and when she does, you will have two problems on your hands: an aggressive, unhappy person in a day program and you will also have to find a residential placement for an unhappy and at times aggressive person because she will not be able to live with us. Or, you can give the funding needed for the proposed courier service."

He did stand up at the meeting. He handed out a copy of what he read to all at the table and he had a copy of the letter sent to a few folks higher up the chain of command from those at the meeting. It was clear that the funding for the wages for the driver would be way less than a residential placement for his daughter. The costs to the funder was what was driving them to force her into the day program but it was the potential cost of *not* following the father's idea that made them change their minds.

It's so sad that the young woman's happiness was not a factor in this decision. It had to do with what it would cost if they didn't make the right call. The moral of this story is right can fall the mighty but first you need to know where to hit them, were it is most effective. In theory the funders saved money. Not spending could seem like a good financial decision but this is not always the case. In Brent's situation they spent huge amounts of money with poor results. In the case of the father demanding the right supports for his daughter the decision-makers were forced into making the financially more-prudent conclusion. Just because it is in the best interest of the individual being supported does not ensure the proper outcome will happen. When you can make them understand that it is in "their" (the funders) best interests that the proper decision be made, then you will get the results that you want.

YOU'RE NOT THE BOSS OF ME

"With power comes the abuse of power. And where there are bosses, there are crazy bosses. That's nothing new."

Judd Rose

This next story involves advocacy and deception from both sides. I was told that I had to attend a meeting at the ministry office in the middle of the following week. I asked what the meeting was about. I was told to just to show up. I said something along the lines of, "I was born at night but not last night." I explained that they had an advantage over me: they knew what the meeting was about and could prepare, I couldn't do the same. I said that I would not attend this scheduled meeting until I knew the agenda.

I had an idea that it was to do with Brent's funding or even a change in his living situation to cut costs. I stood my ground: no agenda no meeting. The social worker at the time tried to intimidate me by saying, "We don't have to tell you what it's about," and something like, "We are the funders and you have to do want we tell you." I said that I did not buy that logic and would wait for the agenda before I would agree to show up. I hung up and a few minutes later I got a call from the social worker. He said the meeting was regarding Brent's home and the costs relating to this residential situation. I thanked him for the information and I would be glad to attend. I then went on to tell him that I had just received a call from Jodi Paterson, the woman who recently did the two newspaper articles on Brent. I said that she wants to meet the day after this ministry meeting was scheduled to see how Brent's life is going and perhaps do a follow-up story. There was silence on the other end of the phone. I broke the silence by asking the exact time and place of this meeting he wanted me to attend. His reply was, "I'll get back to you on that." He never got back to me nor did Jodi call me. She had left the country about a month earlier and was no longer a reporter but the social worker did not know that.

There are two things that those in power are afraid of, lawyers and the media. Getting ether one of them involved, when you have a legitimate concern, can stop their intimidation tactics right in their tracks!

THEY DON'T WANT A COOKIE:

"To say nothing is saying something. You must denounce things that you are against or one might believe that you support things you really do not."

Germany Kent

It's sad that this funder would continue to use bully tactics to browbeat parents into accepting their decisions on how much funding support they would give. I was asked to assist two elderly parents of a son with a developmental disability to sit in on a meeting where they were asking for a little extra funding. A few hours a week was all they were wanting. Their son had moved out of their home a few years prior to live in a group-home setting. The son's father's health was failing and he was wanting this extra funding so a paid person could accompany his son to the weekly sporting events that he so loved to attend. These parents just wanted to have this continue when the time came that they could not do it anymore.

Attending the meeting were the social worker, the parents, myself and the group-home manager. The social worker started the meeting by telling us where the money comes from: the taxpayers. He continued to explain that there was no extra money for this sort of thing and that the parents should be glad for the support their son was getting. He built up his point by saying, "There are some parents who are getting no funding at all." This was a common tactic to shut up parents. I have been told from other families that some social workers have made them feel guilty about having a son or daughter with a disability.

After he was done with explaining that there was no money and they should not ask for more I spoke up. I thanked him for his education on where the money comes from. I said that as long as he'd brought up taxpayers' money I would like to educate him on a few things. I explained that 36 years ago when their son was born these parents had a choice: they could have given him to the state and he would have been placed in Glendale, but they chose to raise him at home. I said that during his tirade I did some rough math. Based on a low estimate of the cost to live in an institution would be in the range of $50,000 a year. Multiplying that by 36 years would come to approximately $1.8 million that the taxpayers did not have to spend. The social worker slammed his book shut and acted insulted this I believe this was done to stop me from continuing, I continued. My closing argument went like this: these parents don't want a cookie for keeping their son at home for 36 years. They just want a few crumbs now to know that he will be able to experience the things in the community to which he was accustomed.

He again showed signs of being indignant and said, "I will see what I can do." Then the meeting was over. Everyone left the room and he stopped me at the door and said, "I am going to tell my manager the things you said at this meeting." My reply was, "Hey why don't I come with you and tell her myself just so you get it right."

THEY NEED US MORE THAN WE NEED THEM

"If you are not making someone else's life better, then you're wasting your time. Your life becomes better by making other's lives better."

Will Smith

Every few years a new funding contract must be signed. I received a call on a Monday morning from the funder. She said that I had to quickly come in and sign for Brent's home contract. I arrived a few hours after the call and asked, "Why the rush to sign." I was told that it should have been signed a few months prior but they forgot to tell me it was ready to have my signature attached. So after I did my scribble she informs me that they will send it right away to get the process going as soon as possible. I enquired, "This won't interrupt when we get the cheque will it?" Turns out it would hamper the timing of the funds arriving. She said that, after the contract gets to the finance department, we would be looking at eight to ten weeks before our organization would get the funding. I said that I would have to call my bookkeeper to see if this would be a problem. I called and was told that it would be a problem, we needed the money by the coming Friday to make payroll.

After getting this information I called the funder and said that it was not acceptable to have this delay and we needed it in four days. I got the same response, there was no way it would arrive before eight weeks and probably closer to ten weeks. She was pleasant and matter of fact in her reply and confident in her timeline of our funds arrival.

I was also matter-of-fact and pleasant in my reply to her. I said, "If we don't receive the money by Friday then you can expect to have us drop off Brent to your office at 3 p.m. that day." I informed her that we were paid for our day support (Monday to Friday 9 a.m. to 3 p.m.) but residentially we would have no money to pay staff. I went on to tell her that come Monday morning we would show up at her office and collect Brent to provide the service for which we are being paid to do.

"You can't do that," was the panicked reply. I said, "I can and I will." I told her of how I was contacted by her office a few years back to come and provide support for an individual whose contractor had a funding beef and just left him at their office. I bailed them out and came in and took him off their hands. I told her that when I arrived at the office the staff were feeding him old Halloween candy to keep him occupied. I told her that at that time she needed me more than I needed the extra work and this would also be the case that Friday. I said that I would give her names and numbers of some people who I thought could bail them out in four days.

I knew this person was not the decision-maker and that she was only the messenger. So I had to convince her that she needed to convince those decision-makers above her that I would do what I said I would do. I had heard somewhere that the way to win a knife fight is to convince your opposition that you are willing to use your weapon. I told her to mention my name to those who occupied nicer offices than she was working in and they would know that I meant business.

It was about 20 minutes after I hung up that I got a call from the funder. She said, "What address would you like that cheque couriered to?"

When I told this story to other contractors they were shocked that I would do this. They said that they have never heard of the finance department getting things done so fast. They also said I had guts to threaten them that way, and I was lucky to still have the contract. I reminded of yet another saying from my dad "Even the smallest dog can lift his leg to pee on the tallest building."

I'M JUST A CLICK AWAY

"Nothing will stop you from being creative so effectively as the fear of making a mistake"

John Cleese

I received an emergency call to provide residential support at our day program. The emergency was that this caregiver had a heart attack and might need major surgery.

I went to their home to pick up this individual along with the things needed for a short stay. I got a call that night saying that things were worse than expected and open-heart surgery was needed. The recovery time would be six to eight months. I started working on a longer-term respite solution, I knew of an extra bed at a home that would be just right for this individual and got the ball rolling for this temporary placement.

But first a little context to this situation. This fellow who had the heart issues was not only looking after the person in question he was also looking after his wife who had cancer. His wife had just received a call to say the cheques would not be coming from the funder while her husband was recovering. She was in a panic. She said she could not work and, without this funding, they would lose their house. She was upset and I calmed her and told her that I had a plan.

I contacted the fellow who made the call to the wife and told her that the funding would stop. I explained to him that this couple had been supporting this individual for more than 18 years and this individual was not an easy person to look after; he was prone to mood swings and aggression. I said this couple had taken him into their home, made him part of their family. They referred to him as their son. They had done a wonderful job with an individual who had gone through a few homes due to his challenging behaviour but these two had been successful for almost two decades. He listened politely and when I was done he said, "We don't pay for services that we don't get." I thanked him for his time and hung up.

I waited two days and called again. I asked if he was sticking to his "no service no pay" mindset and he said "yes." I said, "I thought as much, so here's what I have set up: Are you familiar with the GoFundMe?" He was. I went on to say that I, with the help of a graphic-artist friend of mine, had put together a very nice and flashy GoFundMe page. I explained that it was all ready to go. I went on about what I wrote in this call for assistance: the 18 years of great support, the wife with cancer, and that without this funding this couple would lose their home and more importantly, this individual would lose his home. I then asked him, "Who do you think the villain will be in this story?"

Silence on the phone, then he said, "Are you threatening me?" I replied, "No just giving you a heads- up on what was about to happen- professional courtesy. What I *am* doing is advocating for this individual and his family to save his home. I have no interest in causing your organization bad public relations: it just will be the probable fallout." I suggested to him that he should bring this information to his superiors and make sure he mentions my name. I ended it with, "I am one click away from sending it out and when I do the genie will be out of the bottle. I told him that when this happens I was sure of two things:

1. This couple's financial problems will go away and; 2. Your public relations problems will just begin." I told him that I will wait 24 hours for their final decision.

It was 4 p.m. when I hung up and it was around 10 a.m. the next day when I received a call from this social worker saying that the funding would continue. I thanked him for making his decision, all the while with a smile in my voice and on my face.

I did have a graphic artist friend but no page was ready. I was bluffing but also ready to put this plan into action. Again it's not that you hit them it's knowing where to hit them. David hit Goliath in the right spot with a small rock, I think I did the same. Giving them a chance to avoid negative publicity seemed to be a great way to solve this problem.

THE BIRTH OF THE KJOSA SOCIETY

"Unless someone like you care a whole awful lot, nothing is going to get better. It's not."

The Lorax

Things were moving along very well for Brent: The Namaste Society had purchased a house and he moved in. I was about to relax, thinking he will just live his life. But I get a letter from our funder announcing now that Namaste has Brent's contract our income from them is now just over $500,000. This is the threshold that if an organization surpasses it then it triggers the need for this organization to become accredited. I read the letter not quite understanding what it meant. So I did what I always did: I asked for help from those who would know. I called my friend Julie. She worked for a large society in the city. She proceeded to tell me that the Namaste Society would need to meet the many standards that are required by this accreditation body.

Julie said I was calling her at a good time as they were going through this certification process. She told me that it was a huge undertaking. My reply was, "I guess so, because you have a big organization. It should not be such a big deal because we are so small." This was not the case. Julie said, "It doesn't really matter the size of the organization. The amount of effort to comply is the same." She went on to say, "We have to get outside help to get things in order." "This is not something you can do off the side of your desk."

Accreditation and my take on it: A big company that does this certification process comes to the service provider's office and does an internal examination of the program or programs and examines the business practices of the organization. The goal is to make sure that the program being examined has a commitment to quality improvement and they focus on the unique needs of each person the provider serves. During the survey, "the provider must demonstrate that it conforms to a series of rigorous and internationally recognized standards." So this is where I became concerned. The service provider is given, in advance, the list of what they need to do to "conform" to; then they go about conforming. The objective appears to be for the benefit of the individuals supported but really the goal of the agency is to conform to what the accreditation company wants. So, "If a provider has sufficiently demonstrated its conformance to the standards, it earns accreditation."

You see this accreditation business would be expensive and time consuming. Namaste did not have the financial resources and now with a home to run as well as the day program I would be stretching myself very thin. To add the process of accreditation to my plate, well something would snap.

I had to think of something and as is my way, I went to someone smarter than I am. Again, Penny to the rescue.

As mentioned Penny and I would present to students taking the Community Support worker course and I was able to watch her and I saw what made her a great educator. She never answered a question. When a student would ask her what she thought or what she would do, her answer was, "What do you think?" In human services most answers come from the compassion, caring and common sense of the individual. Penny knew the answers must come from within. This is not math or physics but human connection. If she gave an answer it would teach the student very little. What she was teaching was critical thinking.

So when going to Penny with my, "what should I do" question, she gently guided me to the conclusion that a separate society would be an idea, thereby keeping the Namaste Society below the threshold of the accreditation trigger. She also came up with the name of the new society Kjosa. It's the Icelandic word meaning, "To vote, to elect, to listen and to choose." I liked it because I wanted the name to reflect that we allow choice and we listen to those we support, and having the ability to choose is sometimes not as common as it could be for persons with developmental disabilities.

I got a call from someone asking how the preparation for accreditation was going, I just told her, "I had a choice of paying attention to paper or people…I choose people." I never heard back from her.

Starting a new society was way less work, less expensive and less of a drain on my time. When the contract was being transferred to Kjosa from Namaste I was asked by a person in the ministry, "Is this your clever way of avoiding accreditation?" My reply was "No, it was not *my* clever way." I was also able to defend this decision based on the fact that the operation of a 24-hour residential situation was not in the Namaste Society's mandate.

Brent's brother Bruce, his sister Sherry, Rex and I were the Board members and I became the volunteer president of The Kjosa Community Living Society. Separate from Namaste. But the same.

Being an advocate is not something that one has to do alone. Penny was instrumental to how things worked out for Brent. She does not like it when I describe her as a champion to me. I would say that she was to me what spinach was to Popeye. Another quote from Maya Angelou: "Develop enough courage to stand up for yourself and then stand up for someone else." It was Penny who helped me find that courage. When you know that you have such strong help in a fight, one is less intimidated by the opposition. Penny takes no credit for saving Brent from going back to Woodlands but too bad, I am giving it to her anyway! People like Penny are out there, all you have to do is find others to support you, preferably people who have experience standing up for others. If you are in the right others will stand by you in the fight.

HE'S MY BROTHER AND I WANT YOU TO LOVE HIM

"It's not what we have in our life but who we have in our life that matters."

Margret Laurence

I knew that it would be a matter of time before the cost of Brent's home would be an issue and they would come knocking looking for a cheaper way to support him. We had already changed the mandated two-to-one staffing down to one-to-one, cutting the staffing costs in half. Even with these cost cutting measures I knew that it would not get Brent off the radar as he was still above average in support expenditures. I suggested to the funding agency that Brent could and should have a roommate and this would help in getting the per-person expenses down.

This idea was brushed aside by a new social worker in Brent's life. She still had the old Brent in mind when she told me that it would be too dangerous for anyone to move in with Brent. The new social worker was trying to ride two mules with one ass; she wanted to cut costs but refused my idea to do so.

So Brent eventuality got a roommate but this also involved a fight with the funders. I was speaking at a Community Support worker's award ceremony and afterwards I was approached by a mother of a son with a disability. This gentleman was living with his parents and he was ready to leave the nest. This individual also attended the same Namaste day program that Brent did, so he was no stranger to Brent. She knew about Brent's house and asked if I would consider her son moving in with him. I informed her that it was my hope that Brent could get a house-mate but the funder has been against it. I told her that I would inquire about the possibility of this happening.

I made the inquiry and was met with a negative response. The social worker I spoke to, knew the person I was wanting to move in with Brent and said that they would not be a good match. She said that Ian was a "high level" individual. That was somewhat offensive, what was Brent? She also went on to wrongfully describe Brent as a "dangerous guy" and this would put Ian in peril. The parents after meeting Brent felt otherwise. So the fight was on to help these parents, their son and Brent.

The social worker at the time sent me an email explaining the reasons why this proposed placement was a bad idea. I took this email to Penny to ask her advice. The following is the reply that she help me put together;

February 23, 2004

XXXXXX XXXXX

Resource Worker

Community Living Services

Dear XXXXXX,
On January 18th, 2004, I wrote to you to correct some misperceptions presented in your email of January 15th, 2004 regarding my proposal to have a particular individual move into the Goose Home.

I also need to raise the issue of my working relationship with the ministry as described in your note. Your email stated that the space at the Goose house has remained unfilled because of the "...poor working relationship (I) shared with the Provincial Review team and the regional manager afterwards". A review of the PMG report of the Goose house would show that apart from some small housekeeping details, the final report was glowing. As for the alleged poor relationship with the PMG I would disagree. They made recommendations and suggested changes of which we complied with.

Your note also states, "I know this is a convenient placement for you Terry, but what do you think is in Ian's best interests? I am not being rhetorical here...". You seem to imply that I am placing my needs (whatever you perceive these to be) ahead of Ian's. These and other statements in your note raise concern for me. I feel it is essential for us to take a careful look at our roles, to clearly identify issues affecting our relationship and to adopt a more constructive and professional approach to communicating and working in partnership.

In the last few years, several of your colleagues have made claims that I was in violation of my contract with the ministry because of my efforts to advocate and problem-solve on behalf of my clients. These claims were unsubstantiated. I addressed them as they arose, and according to my records, the ministry did not find that I was in violation of my contract. If concerns or questions continue to exist about the Society's fulfillment of its contract then I would request that these be put in writing and forwarded to me at your earliest convenience. We have done our best to be accountable, fair and transparent in our practices. The ministry has also made a commitment to open, accountable and transparent relationships.

Your stated reason for denying that individual and his family the opportunity to explore the Goose House as a possible placement is not based on the quality of support that the Society provides, or on the overall quality of the living environment. As you state in your email "there is recognition that the home has supported (the individual) well, but to be honest, reservations exist another placement (sic)".

Leaving an available vacancy unfilled this long in a time of such limited resources is a very serious matter. It is in everyone's interests that any outstanding issues you perceive regarding our working relationship should be clearly presented and resolved so that our scarce community resources are available to people who need them. I am concerned that these perceptions have unfairly penalized those who most need us to work cooperatively – individuals with disabilities and their families. I look forward to hearing from you soon and to working in partnership with you.

Sincerely,

Terry Flatt

Executive Director

Namaste Transition to Community Society

Again a person in power making a decision based on what was rather than what is. Also not understanding the dynamics of interpersonal relationships. Ian, in some ways functioned "higher" than Brent, in other ways not. This is common to us all. In the case of these two living together it worked, Ian would become literally an extra support for Brent. Ian often assists Brent by giving his arm as support as he is unsteady on his feet. Ian is a helper, wants to contribute when he sees the need. He became an aid for Brent.

Ian spent his first night at the Goose house and things went swimmingly. The next morning Ian and Bent came to the day program and that was when Brent came to me and grabbed my arm and said, "I want you to meet someone." He pulled me over to Ian and says, "This is Ian, he's my brother. I want you to love him. I want you to love him to bits."

THIS IS BRENT'S LIFE

"Difficult roads often lead to beautiful destinations."

Unknown

Brent now has a house manager he calls Momma Her real name is Sheryl and they love each other. Brent has staff who take him to their homes for Christmas dinner, as well as summer BBQ's. It was at one of these BBQ's that Brent brought the house down, not literally but in a funny way. He was introduced to one of his workers boyfriend. Upon being introduced he said "Hey Rick, can I ask you something?" Rick said, "Sure Brent ask away." With a wry smile he says "Rick, have you been an asshole all your life?" This seemed to get the desired results as he had all around him in stiches. Brent is now very social, attends the weekly dance with Ian and he calls Ian's parents Mom and Dad when they come to visit.

Brent is now in a better place but his reputation is still around. I was talking to a person who works in the field of supporting persons with developmental disabilities and she asked me if I knew how Brent was doing. I told her that he is doing great. I wondered why she had inquired after Brent. She told me that when her doctor asked what her profession was and she told her that she was a community- support worker, the doctor asked if she knew what happened to Brent Smith. The doctor had done some work at Glendale to pay her way through medical school. She said she never worked with Brent but he scared the hell out of her. She was given stories of his ability to inflict damage on staff. It seems that this information had a lasting effect on her, seeing as she remembered Brent and his reputation more than 30 years later. I told this woman to please tell her doctor that she need not be scared of Brent anymore… he is a sweetheart!

THE POWER OF RELATIONSHIPS

"To love someone is to strive to accept that person exactly the way he or she is, right here and now-and to go on caring even through times that may bring pain."

Fred Rogers

It takes little insight to see that institutions were less than ideal for persons held captive in them. They ultimately made everyone less than able: They often hurt the people who lived in them and they limited the ability of caregivers to question the system that made the rules. The people who needed help often received hurt instead. They lost their freedom and were living a life void of dignity. This was done under the guise of protecting them.

When we assume that people who are different from the norm have to change, and until that change happens they don't belong in our society, we become the worst kind of protector. We kept others who are "not like us" oppressed, but we did so with the belief we were helping while we did it. Just because the intentions claim to be good, it does not and should not excuse us for irresponsible behavior.

Brent lived at the tail end of the ugly institutional days. He received corporal punishment for being different and not taking this oppression lying down. Brent was the most troublesome of the oppressed; he fought back. As the Woodlands staff said to Brent's sister, *"he gives as good as he gets."* I suggest that when he was nine, in Woodlands, he got more than he gave.

Brent received a three-year lesson in Woodlands on violence and how aggression could be used against him as well as for him. Bringing these lessons to a new and improved Glendale institution proved to be a big problem for those supporting him. The good thing about this change in environment for Brent was he turned the tables and began to give way more than he got. I suspect there were isolated incidents at Glendale where after a staff having taken a blow or two from Brent might have given one in return, but with the new and more humane culture at Glendale, physical payback was rare.

Perhaps the biggest injustice to Brent was not so much the lack of *understanding* of why he was violent, it was the lack of *interest* in trying to understand why. Those in power would revert to the old-school idea of controlling and correcting the incidents of dangerous behaviour with any means that the behaviour professionals knew of, such as chemical or physical restraints. This would result in having little or no long-term effects in eliminating the behaviour. It just showed a lack of imagination. If the only tool you have is a hammer then all the problems look like nails. They tried only what they knew and looked no further than what they could easily see. They should have realised that what they were doing was not working and sought another way. They never found another way. How could they? It seemed that they never bothered to look.

When Brent was living in the day program, my 12-year-old son and I stopped by on a Sunday morning to visit him. Upon leaving, my son questioned why Brent was living there. I told him that where he was living before, they were trying to control him and Brent did not take kindly to that control. My son seemed to think about it for a moment then said, "If you want to control someone you should give them some control first." A smart thing to say…must get that from his mother.

The other avenue that was never explored was the power of relationships. There were some staff at Glendale that "got" Brent and had formed a relationship with him. Without a real relationship, it is almost impossible to be able to properly understand someone.

Hindsight is easy and often clear but why did those doing the behaviour programing not seek more real input from those who had an understanding of Brent? They would have been the best people to guide others in supporting him. Why did someone, in an office far away from Brent, after reading reports about him, not ask the direct hands-on staff on the best way to provide support? I ask the questions having the answer. It is just the hierarchy of the institutional system: those with the qualifications know best!

Giving considerable weight to an academically trained professional's opinions and giving little or no weight to the opinions of a person who has a good relationship with the individual was ineffective. Years of hands-on experience with a subject can have more value than textbook theory. This, in some cases, still exist, in community living.

Taking Brent out of the institution did not mean this backwards thinking changed. I suggest it got worse for Brent as he was even more isolated, with no one around him who understood him. The hierarchy in the community seemed to be the same. The educated psychologist and an inexperienced social worker were calling the shots with no real understanding of who Brent was as a person. With this lack of knowledge they would widely miss the mark of helping Brent. When these ideas failed, they just loaded up with more ammunition of what was not working and fired away.

To quote Herb Lovett from his Learning to Listen book, *"Technologies to control behaviour fail to ask people why they do something and without that vital information, we find ourselves trying to control something we do not properly understand. Because hitting another person is a serious matter, we might better respond to it seriously, not mechanically. If a person is automatically timed-out for hitting, then we are regimenting ourselves when we could be thinking flexibly about constructive options. Regaining control is part of this process, not the point of it. Most people get upset for a reason and we need to find what that is, if we are really going to help. But if a person is so upset that we cannot determine the reason immediately, then making the situation less tense is a first step. It is asking too much of anyone to be angry and articulate at the same time."*

In the Namaste day program, whenever there is a situation where a person becomes upset, agitated or aggressive we look for ways to reassure the person that we are there to help them through this time. We then ask them and ourselves, "What did we miss?" We ask this because we must have missed something. We don't blame, chastise or punish the behaviour. That only makes matters worse. In almost all challenging behaviour what is being said by the one presenting this behaviour is that *something is wrong in my world*, and our job is to find out what that something is.

If we decide that the main goal is to eliminate the behaviour then we effectively are telling that person, "If you communicate that way we will not listen." Too often, when a person displays challenging behaviour we say, "Calm down, then we will help." This is backwards thinking. It is like saying to a person who is drowning, "as soon as you learn to swim we will rescue you." Helping or showing that we want to help, is what leads to calm. When Brent, at the Pink house, communicated that something was wrong, the help, with misguided instructions, walked and sometimes ran away.

MUCH LIKE US

"Don't concern yourself with the opinion of those who judge you. That is placing on them an importance they do not have."

Donna Lynn Hope

He's an example of how out-of-touch some of the most senior decision-makers were and how little they know of the disability community. I attended a meeting in or around 2005. The funding agency, was to make some announcements to a room of community living contractors and other community stakeholders. After a bunch of information about changes like new office location and other things that I had no interest in, they revealed their new promotional tools. The idea was to put up posters, for the general public, to help them get to know persons with developmental disabilities and to foster a better understanding of these folks. It was a good idea in as much as the general public could use some education regarding persons with developmental disabilities. These folks were somewhat new in the real world. The first poster was of a smiling middle-aged man who had facial features contorted somewhat, and he looked different, or how a person in the general public would think a person with a disability would look like. The tagline under this photo was, "Just Say Hi." I did not mind this education tool. Having spent my formative years in a mill town where there were very few persons with developmental disabilities. Some of my friends from this town have told me that they don't know how to interact when they meet a person with a developmental disability and I also gave them the advice of, "just say hi and see what happens."

Now after the "Say Hi" poster was proudly presented they brought out another one. This one featured a teenaged girl, with Down syndrome. Her hair was the same color of the Golden Retriever she was hugging. The tagline to this poster was, "persons with developmental disabilities have hopes and dreams much like us." Now words have meaning and when they are strung together it can tell a lot about who put them in that order. Not sure if all in the room saw what I did. I was sitting next to Penny and I knew she saw it. I whispered, "How could they write that?" Her reply was "because that must be what they think."

A few weeks later I was speaking at a conference and the funder had an information table there. The woman behind the table was looking bored and seemed relieved that I made eye contact with her and was heading her way. She had, on the wall behind her, both those posters. I asked if I could have a closer look at the one with the young woman and the dog. She took it off the wall and placed it on the table in front of me. I took a pen and drew a thin line through the word, "much". I told her that this would make this poster more educational because persons with developmental disabilities don't have hopes and dreams "much" like us, they have hopes and dreams "just" like us. This was like Dr. Goodard in the early 1900s calling persons with developmental disabilities, "the almosts." They were "almost" like us and the top brass in the funding agency seemed to think the same way-they are not *almost* like us they now are "much" like us. Just a slight improvement.

They seem to have thought that persons with developmental disabilities were much like us because after reading these 11 words they let it get printed. It somehow did not cause them to think that these words did the opposite of what they were hoping to do. What it did was to continue the belief that persons with developmental disabilities were so different that they are not the same as us! The fact is that persons with developmental disabilities are different as am I to any other person. This fact gets lost when the focus is on the differences and ignore the things that make us the same: I want to be loved and to love. I want to be kept warm, safe and dry. I want good food and good company and I want to do things that interest me. These are the huge similarities that persons with developmental disabilities have with those without a developmental disability.

I was being interviewed by a newspaper about the Namaste Friday music program where more than 250 persons with developmental disabilities attend each week. This event is unique as it is geared for persons with developmental disabilities, where four professional musicians are the backup band for those who want to sing their songs of choice. (Google, "Global News Namaste music," for an idea of this event.)

This reporter asked me, "What does music mean to those who attend?" I asked her; what does music mean to anyone, even if they don't have a developmental disability? They are us; we are them. We are all just a bump in the head away from needing the supports that persons with developmental disabilities need. We are all only temporarily able.

Judging the funders efforts to educate the public about persons with developmental disabilities, I suggest that it was the folks in this agency that needed to be educated. After putting that line though the word "much" on that poster I think it got back to the powers that be and I never saw that poster again.

MORE MAGIC WATER

"Those who don't believe in magic will never find it."

Unknown

Due to this success of making changes to Brent's environment, as well as changes to the attitudes of those supporting him, I have been asked on numerous occasions by other agencies to help in similar situations. One such situation was with Brad. He had been placed in Woodlands at the age of 12 in 1970. He spent two years behind the walls of Woodlands. In 1972, instead of being placed in Glendale, he was placed in a congregate community setting in Victoria.

Brad was a tall and gentle guy, compliant and well behaved. Brad was about 45 years old when I first met him. He was well over six feet tall and weighed more than 250 pounds. He had been ramping up his agitation and it had been spilling out into aggression. The house staff were scared of him, as were his roommates of many years. For the last ten years at this home Brad had never had any anger or aggression issues.

I was asked to help better understand this behavicural change by the agency operating his home. I explained how I work; I needed time to get to know Brad, to try to form a relationship with him and with his caregivers. I spent 16 hours a day with Brad for two weeks straight. I was working as one of the team in his home and day-work program. Brad had some vocabulary but he was not a talkative guy. He is autistic and not very expressive. During my time with Brad and his supporters I wanted to see how he was being supported, to see how he communicated his frustrations and I hoped to learn what those frustrations were.

There was one incident that gave me some insight to understanding Brad. It was after dinner and Brad was having a bath. I was upstairs, chatting with the home staff. Brad had just gotten out of the tub when I heard the commotion; loud screaming from him. I ran down the stairs to see the staff fleeing towards the office and Brad standing naked in his bedroom yelling, "It hurts, it hurts." Now a big part of my strategy, in these things, was to not do what was in the behavior protocol, because it was not working. The protocol was to get him a pill, a calming drug of choice. So after seeing the staff run for the pill, I did the opposite. Walking into Brad's room where he was complaining about pain and clinching his stomach. I went right up to him and asked where it hurt. I am no hero and I was a bit apprehensive of this man who outweighed me by 100 pounds. He was extremely agitated and I do not blame staff for running away. I just knew that leaving Brad was not helpful to him.

I told him very calmly that I was here to help and I asked him to show me where it hurt. Brad pointed to his stomach. I did the thing that doctors do you know- the thumping of the cupped hand with the other hand-on his stomach. Brad then changed the location of the pain to his head. I realized I needed a change in my doctor routine and said to him, "Come with me." I held his hand and led him back to the bathroom across the hall. I turned on the cold water in the sink and asked him to lean down towards the sink. I told Brad that this was magic water and cupped some and sort of sprinkled it over his head. I guess I went from playing doctor to playing priest. After one dose of magic water Brad asked for "more magic water." One more sprinkle and Brad said, "All better, all better."

I looked up to see the staff at the door with a glass of water and a small cup with the pills. I said to the staff that I didn't think the pills were needed but he could use the water. Brad drank the water and we went back to his room and he put on his pajamas and went to bed with no other concerns.

I noticed during my time with Brad that the staff's interaction with him was verbal, no physical contact or physical interaction. He did not seek out touch so perhaps he did not want to be touched. I wanted to test this theory. I had a short encounter with him after picking him up from a family member's house after a holiday meal. I asked him what he had for dinner and he said, "Turkey." I asked him where it went he said, "My tummy", I patted him on his ample belly and I saw a slight smile but it was ever so slight. I made another attempt at touch while he was having his snack at the kitchen table. I was chatting with one of his staff when I started to gently punch his back, like they do when you get a massage. He gave no reaction positive or negative so I continued till my arms got tired. When I stopped he looked up at me then took my arm and placed my hand on his back. I said, "no it's my turn," so he gave me one light punch to my back then again placed my hand on his back to indicate that he liked this contact. This was passed on to the staff that he indeed liked the human touch, he just didn't show it.

The reason I tell this story is because I believed Brad was communicating that he needed help. But with his size and now reputation all it did was cause this help to leave. He got the opposite of what he was looking for. Again I am not blaming the staff for their actions when Brad was in this state. He was scary but his intent was not to frighten. When one interprets a behaviour to mean something, and if the guess is wrong then our reaction is also wrong. We then go down a trail that is leading us away from the solution. The sooner we realize we are going in the wrong direction the better. However, more often than not, those in power that choose the direction tend to hang on to that choice harder and longer than they should. I heard a quote that said, "It's much easier to fool someone than it is to convince them that they have been fooled." In the case of how to best support others it is hard to convince the decision-makers that their methods or ideas are wrong.

I was able to help change the staffs' attitude toward what Brad's behaviour was telling them. When they reacted differently towards his agitated behaviour, the behavior changed. Like Brent, they needed to not feel scared and understand that it was Brad who was scared about something and that their job was to console him through his fears. They were a great bunch of people who cared deeply for him and they jumped at the chance to help. He remained in his home and, with a change in attitude and action by the staff, he went back to being that big gentle person he was in the past.

CHANGE COMES FROM WITHIN

"You have your way. I have my way. As for the right way, the correct way, and the only way, it does not exist"

Friedrich Nietzhe

This is the method I used to help Brad's support team come to see that his behavior for what it was - a cry for help.

The old joke goes like this: a Buddhist monk asks for a hot dog from a street vendor in New York. He says to the vendor, "Make me one with everything." The vendor does just that and hands the monk his hot dog with the works. The monk hands the vendor a $20 bill and he promptly puts the bill in his pocket. The monk waits for change from the vendor but nothing. The monk says to him, "What about the change?" He quickly replies, "You should know better than most, change comes from within."

That's what I needed to do with those supporting Brad. I needed to change how they saw Brad and It had to come from within themselves. Too often in these situations someone comes into the picture, someone thought to be an expert, and observes a bit then tells everyone what they need to do or need to change. This can have mixed results. Telling someone to "see things my way" or "do things the way I say to do it" without getting the "buy in" can lead to undesirable results.

My plan was to get the staff to talk about themselves - not a hard thing to do as most people are more than happy to talk about themselves and tell you what they think.

There were about 15 people at this in-service. I split them up into three groups and asked them to come up with answers to these questions: If they were in need of support from someone else, to help you when you are experiencing physical pain, emotional pain, anxiety or frustration, how do you want to be supported during these times?

They all went into their groups and started to discuss and write down their preferred ways of being supported - the things that were helpful as well as the things that were not helpful. They came back and presented their thoughts to the group.

When being supported with physical pain most wanted:

- Pain relief.

- Confidence that the person supporting them that knew what he or she was doing

- That until the pain was manageable the support person should not leave them.

When it came to the question of emotional pain, anxiety and frustration the following were the main things they wanted in support:

- Being believed that what they feel is real.

- They want to be listened to, not talked to.

- To not be told "Here's what I would do."

- To not have their feelings dismissed or told not to feel that way.

The staff needed little encouragement to describe how they wished to be supported when in these types of distress.

I had them where I wanted - expressing their feelings and opening up about themselves. And this took only about 45 minutes and during this time I never mentioned Brad's name once because it was not about him, it was about them.

After all presentations were given I asked them some questions, knowing the answers. "Do you care about Brad?"

Yes they all replied. "Do you believe that behavior is communication?" "Yes," again. "Can we all agree that Brad has the same emotions and feelings as we all do?" "Yes."

I said, "Great, then if Brad is communicating that something is wrong in his world and his behaviour is asking – no - pleading, for help then we should provide that help and do so in the way we would desire, the ways we had voiced and written down.

For Brad, like Brent, the focus was on his behaviour. It was frightening, it was intimidating, but it was not seen as asking for help. This was the shift for the staff; they needed this shift to come from within, and they just needed a little help in having it come out. Oh, and the staff also integrated playful touch with Brad something that he really liked and something that they had no idea about.

With Brent, running away (i.e., the evacuation procedure) was exactly the opposite of what he needed. We often fail those we wish to help when we don't take into account the sensibilities and sensitivities of these people whose behaviour is of concern. When we objectively observe people we can gain some insight, like baseline data and such, but in doing so we lose the subjective impressions. We also need to spend more time analyzing our own behaviour so that our intentions don't differ from our actions.

When there is no mutual respect, the only right is might. Where there is no love, power becomes the object of desire for both the giver of support and the receiver of the support. Brent wanted some power, some control. Those who supported him in the past also wanted the power and control. This was the perfect storm for conflict and Brent was not willing to concede anything.

Things are very good for Bent now. He has people around him who understand him. There was this wonderful woman named Lillian who had a brother who was leaving Glendale. The ministry had a form for her to fill out regarding her brother's needs. There was one question that read, "What can your family member learn?" She put a line through the word "learn" and wrote "teach" in its place. We as care-givers sometimes think we must do the teaching and when we do that we tend to forget what we can learn. I heard a saying; "I will learn nothing today by talking, it is only when I listen do I learn." When we began to listen to Brent he became a good teacher.

THE HOCKEY TURTLENECK SWEATER

"Because you take away a man's freedom of choice, even his freedom to make the wrong choice, is to manipulate him as though he was a puppet on a string."

Madeline L'Engle

Brent, for his own reasons, becomes attached to objects. He would insist that he only have his coffee in a "Timmy's" cup from Tim Hortons. This moved to "the blue" one. These tended to run their course but when he was in this frame of mind it was easier to allow him these choices. I suspect this was due to his inability for many years to have few if any choices in his life.

This brings me to the hockey turtleneck sweater as Brent came to call this item of clothing. I stored my hockey equipment in a closet in my office at work. This is for the betterment of my relationship with my wife, as airing out my gear at home could be grounds for divorce.

Brent was visiting me in my office and he took a shine to my hockey sweater hanging up in the closet. He got his hands on it and it became his. I had other sweaters so this one could be spared for him. It soon became the only thing he would wear. It got to a point where he would sit on a chair in front of the washer and dryer till the cleaning and drying process was done as it seemed that he did not want this item out of his sight.

It soon began to fall apart and he made the decision to throw it away but up until that time this hockey turtleneck was a thing of great worth to him.

When we, as support people, think it is our job to teach those in our charge we often disregard, ignore or just don't see what we can learn. Too often we think we know what is best for "them." We need to get over ourselves. We need to allow real choices, not just the choices we think they should make. It is said we learn from our mistakes and if you are a person with a disability we tend to keep a close eye on them to jump in and herd them away from what we feel is a bad decision by them.

I was told a story about an adult woman with a developmental disability, who wanted to buy a G-string. This woman was discouraged from making this purchase. Finally a staff spoke up and said, "This is her decision and she has her own money. I'll take her to get one." Off they went. The purchase was made and upon the return home she went to her bedroom to try it on. It did not take long before she came out and said, "What a stupid thing."

In hindsight it was not a wise purchase and I understand that G-strings, after trying them on, it cannot be returned. However, it was wise to allow her to learn that herself, to not get in her way. There are times when we try to shield those we support, but in doing so we stunt instead.

Persons with developmental disabilities often have well-meaning folks get in their way and they are mostly polite when we do. I suggest that if we had someone consistently getting in our way or judging what we should be "allowed" to do, this someone would soon be told, in a less-than-polite way, to piss off.

I am sure we have all heard, "Here's what you should do," even when you have not asked for an opinion. I remember overhearing a conversation in a restaurant. The owner of this new establishment was taking an order from a customer. Wanting to be helpful, the customer said, "I really like your restaurant but you know what *you* should do?" And before he could finish his words of wisdom the owner interrupted him and said, "You know what you should do is start a consulting business so if I want your opinion on what I should do with my business then I can give you a call. Now what would you like to order?" Pretty sure he did not get a tip but, hey, he owned the joint.

I suggest that the owner of that restaurant was fed up with others telling him what he should do. For persons with developmental disabilities the same is true. It is not that simple for these folks to find a clever way of reacting to the constant herding, the constant being told what to do. Take Pete, the fellow who wore the tube restraints to bed. He was a big guy but he did not put up any sort of a fuss when putting on this apparatus. I suspect he did not like wearing the restraint and perhaps he did not cooperate at the beginning. This non-compliance would have been met with force so he probably just resigned himself to the fact that others had the power and he was powerless. Why "fight a fight that can't be won," seemed to be Pete's way of dealing with this inequity. Brent dealt with it differently, he was willing to fight regardless of a losing outcome.

Brent, like all of us, wanted to be treated fairly; he wanted honesty; and he wanted to be listened to. An example of this desire for honesty was the time Brent was set to leave the day program and go back to the Goose house. On his way out I said my goodbyes. Brent stopped and looked at me and said, "You fucking liar." I was taken aback but then I remembered earlier in the day I had told him I would take him out for coffee. Something came up and I forgot my promise. I then told the Goose house staff that I would deliver Brent home as I had a promise to keep.

LEAKY EYES

"Every day may not be good, but there is something good in every day."

Unknown

I'd like to offer another example of how Brent's ability to experience the same emotions as all of us was underestimated. Brent was at the day program and having a particularly bad day. He was mad about something and in the past he would hit others but he moved on from that and was hitting himself instead. This was in the early stage of getting his new home set up. I was up to my neck in the paper and planning. These were things I preferred not to do and I, like Brent, was frustrated. But I was not hitting myself. Anyway, it was brought to my attention that Brent was in need of my time. When Brent was like this I was the go-to guy to help him through his frustration. I had to drop what I was doing and tend to his needs.

Off we go in my truck, my mind being elsewhere. I thought I was hiding it but Brent knew. His verbal rage changed and it was directed towards me: "Fuck you, Flattie," he yelled. I snapped and did something I have never done before during these situations: I reacted negatively. Normally, my reaction to this would be tossing back the opposite that was being thrown at me calm: to frantic, polite to rude. I pulled the truck over and I went off, "No. You fuck you." I went on a long rant, telling him the list of things I had on my plate because of him. My worries about the potential of delayed funding and needing to take out a personal bank loan to meet payroll, and the hours spent fighting the ministry to keep him here. "No, you fuck you Brent."

When I was done, Brent was silent and did not say a word on our drive back to the program. At least he stopped hitting himself, I thought. As I pulled up, Karen came out to help get Brent back to the program. I left the truck and passing Karen, I said, "I lost it on him."

Then I was back in my office with my frustrations about the administrative tasks. About 10 minutes went by. I was just getting immersed into the paper when Karen came in and told me, "There is someone here who wants to talk to you." I did not need another distraction. I got up from my desk and went to the door. Standing there is Brent, keys in hand looking down at his feet. He looks up and says, "I'm sorry, Flattie." This made my eyes leak a little bit and I said, "I'm sorry too." We hugged each other for a long time. Brent then went on to have a good day. I went on with a new understanding of how much Brent understood about me and how much I did not realize about him.

This was not the first time Brent apologized to me. During a period when he was coming to the day program seven days a week. Brent arrived on that Saturday in soiled pants. He was experiencing cramps and was not only foul smelling but was understandably in a foul mood. His anger and his fists were directed at me. I was able to avoid being hit, just by moving away from him. During his attempts to strike he was also spitting venom, "I'll kill you Flattie. I hate you." My replies were "I love you, Brent." "How about I clean you up." This time I did it the right way. This anger and attempted aggression lasted for about an hour and I could see I was wearing him down. Negativity has a tough time living in a room full of positive. Finally he said, "Could you clean him up Flattie." I asked for a promise that he would not try to hit me and that promise was made.

The tub was run and after the cleanup was over and new clothes put on I went about getting lunch ready. Brent was walking about the place playing with his keys, when he came up to me and said, "How about some sugar?" Which means he wanted a hug. I gave him some sugar. That was when he whispered in my ear, "Flattie, could you fix him, could you fix his brain." I told him, "Brent, if I did that I would be out of a job." He then asked me, "Do you love me Flattie." I said, "I love you, Brent, I love you like a brother." I think this was his way of saying he was sorry. Asking if I loved him was his way of asking for forgiveness. He knew what he had done and understood that I didn't deserve what he was handing out. This is a clear indication that he was always aware of what was being handed to him except this time it was positive.

UNDERSTANDING, NOT PATIENCE

"Speak in such a way that others love to listen to you. Listen in such a way that others love to speak to you."

Anonymous

I have had many people say to me, "You must have a lot of patience to do this." My reply was always, "A carpenter has patience. Carpentry frustrates me because sometimes I will cut a board twice and it's still too short." This attempt at analogy and humor was due to the fact that I had little patience for carpentry. When building something, I just wanted to get to the finished product and did not understand the importance of doing the little things right, taking the time to make sure it is level or plumb. With this lack of understanding my end product was a joke. "If I build it they will laugh." After inspecting the treehouse I built for my kids, my dad remarked, "Well if you were galloping by on a horse at 50 yards you would have no idea that this thing is not level."

I was helping my friend, Cam, a carpenter, on a renovation project. I observed how he would take his time to make things right before hammering the nail or drilling the screw. I would say, "That's good enough." I was soon schooled on the folly of "good enough" and how it will come back and bite you in the ass. He said, "Do it right and you will only have to do it once."

So after my education in carpentry I was being interviewed by some university students about the work I do. When the common query came up regarding patience I went to the standard answer, then stopped myself. I told them that a carpenter does not have patience. My friend Cam does not have patience for faulty power tools. I recollect a time when a drill stopped working. First, he unplugged it. Then whipped it around like a hammer-toss competition and flung the drill into the pond close by. I suspect that in 50 years when the pond gets drained and condos are built they will find this primitive tool and wonder how it got there.

The point I am trying to make is Cam clearly did not have patience for a faulty drill. However when it came to carpentry he had an understanding of what needed to be done to get the desired results…a sound, strong structure. In my work, I also have an understanding of what needs to be done to help the person I am supporting, to communicate their needs, their concerns and frustrations. If I try to rush this communication, or misunderstand what their behaviour is trying to tell me, I would only add to this person's frustrations, resulting in the opposite of my desired outcome. If we take the time to do it right we only have to do it once. Too often, in our rush for a solution to a problem involving challenging behaviour, we don't take the time to fully understand; that's when we make mistakes. We not only disrespect the person we are hoping to help, we hinder as well.

The best way or perhaps the only way to understand a person's behaviour is to listen to what the behaviour is saying. The Chinese phrase, "to listen" has three characters, *eyes, ears and heart*. If you don't use all three then a poor translation will happen. With your ears you listen to the tones: are they sad, angry, or frustrated. With your eyes, what do you see in their face? What do you see in their body language? What do you see in their environment? With your heart, how do you show that you hear them? How do you show that you are making the effort to listen? These efforts communicate back to the individual that you care and want to help. This leads to calmness of the person and this calmness leads to this person's ability to better express what their problem is so it can properly be addressed. I had the chance for a teaching moment for a new staff. Mitch was putting on Brent's shoes, while this was going on I was conversing with this new staff. In the middle of our conversation Brent said something to Mitch, used his name and asked him a question. Mitch, perhaps thinking that he needed to listen to me seeing as I was his boss, ignored Brent's question. I was quick to point out the importance of listening to Brent when he reaches out to you with his words. When he makes it clear that he has something to say to you, you should listen. If you ignore him he will feel that it is not necessary to listen to you. I let Mitch know that this is one of the keys to building a proper relationship with anyone, Brent included. Show him respect then you got him; show him otherwise and, he's gone.

HAPPY PEOPLE DON'T HIT

"Happiness is the richest thing we will ever own"

Donald Duck

I was speaking at a conference and the title of my talk was Happy People Don't Hit. I was scheduled to speak at 2 p.m. I started off by saying: for those of you attending this talk and wanting to bring back some words of wisdom to your organizations but would rather take off and get started on your beer consumption-I will give you a condensed version of what I am going to talk about. When it comes to people who display challenging behaviour we need to find out what they like…do plenty of that. We need to find out what they don't like…don't do any of that. Two guys wrote this down and left.

The remainder of my talk was mostly on the importance of relationship building. When a person who is challenging to support and his or her verbal communication is limited or non-existent, it is the positive relationships that can communicate to everyone. Only when the relationship is created can we have a better chance to find out what they like and what they don't like. I received a written comment after the talk and it said, "A very simplistic solution to a complex problem." I would have liked to have had that comment during my talk. I would have explained that yes, the words are simple; it was the creation of an equitable relationship that is hard. There are people working in this field that feel they are not equals with those they support. If they believe this, the only relationship they have with those they support is one of power and control. The supporter has the power and control and the person being supported does not.

Most challenging behavior is due to a person attempting to regain some power and control. Some staff feel that the person they are supporting needs to change and once they do, things will be better for them both.

I was looking at a relationship book in the bookstore and the first line of the book said, "If you are not willing to accept half the responsibility for the problems in your relationship, then don't bother to read any further." We need to look at what we are doing and see if we change something in ourselves, could that change someone else's behaviour?

Buddha teaches: "Rarely is it the problem that will cause us the most grief…it is often how we react to the problem that does." In the case of challenging behaviour, hitting others, hitting themselves, yelling, or destruction to the environment, we as support people have two things to focus on: 1. stopping the behavior; 2. figure out what the behavior is communicating to us. The behaviour that I have noted can be scary. There is often a safety issue involved-a chance for injury to persons displaying it and to those around them. Safety is important but perhaps in our stampede towards making things safe we wear blinders, focusing on only making things safe. If we take them to the ground, hold their arms and legs so the potential of injury or environmental destruction is contained, then our job is done…safety achieved. I am not saying that restraint during these times is always wrong but could a different approach to the situation be explored? In the case of a random person in the public behaving erratically, police are called. They come upon this stranger; they have no idea who they are. All they see is a behaviour, and have no idea what led up to it. Their focus is on the safety of the person and those in the vicinity.

In the world of supporting persons with developmental disabilities we know these people or we should know them. I will say that it's been my experience that before persons with developmental disabilities behave in extreme ways, they give signs that they are heading in that direction. Sometimes these signs at subtle; other times they are clear and concise: "I don't want to go swimming!" When these signs are not noticed due to inexperience, not paying attention or just ignoring the verbal or behavioural cues, these negative situations will happen.

"You love swimming. Grab you bag and get in the van!" Then they wonder why they had a meltdown at the pool.

We as support workers need to consider whether our reactions help our clients, have their concerns been met or heard or are we just meeting our concerns?

I saw an incident recently where the reaction to a situation made things worse than it had to be. A support person was sitting in the last row of seats at our weekly music event. A young, mid 20s man with a developmental disability, gave a light tap to the back of this persons head. This young man knew this staff and it seemed to be done in a playful manner. This supporter stood up quickly and showed anger for this act. This person did not go to the individual that tapped his head, he went right to this individual's worker. The offended support person explained how inappropriate this action was and demanded something be done about it. This set into motion the following: The direct support staff brought the perpetrator to the inconvenienced person and demanded that he apologize for his breach of proper behavior. This individual did not take kindly to this demand: he dug his heels in and yelled, "NO!" This set off his support person to say that they must leave the event. Not sure the reason he had to leave. Was it because he raised his voice? Was it because he was non-compliant to the demand for an apology?" Whatever the reason for this explosion, the complaining staff person got his pound of flesh.

The reaction to this harmless, playful touch caused a blow-up and removal of this individual from a place where until then he was having a great time. The perceived foul was small, the reaction was over the top and the grief to the individual who was banished was huge.

When we don't look at our reactions to a situation and only take into account the actions of the individual we are supporting, we lose half the equation. We, as support people, write up the "incident" reports and rarely do we say, "I could have handled it better." Instead, we point the finger to the person receiving the support. The old line that says "When you are pointing a finger at another, there are three fingers pointing right back at you.

As support people we make mistakes-many of them and until we start to admit or think about what we did or didn't do to contribute to the incident we will make the same mistakes over again and while those we support will suffer. The line to an old blues song "Before you accuse me, take a look at yourself," is good advice.

When I speak at a class for students wanting to work in this field I tell them that they will have power over those they will be supporting. Like a superhero, you must use this power for good, not evil. I believe that wielding this power for one's own benefit is evil. Demanding that those they support, "Do as I say" is unjust. Making someone conform to how you think they should behave is just wrong.

Think before you speak, act or direct. Is what I am doing fair to the individual? Where will my actions lead, how will they react, will this have a positive ending?

Too often the individual's problem becomes secondary. In Brent's case it was more the problem it caused staff, the psychologist and the support system. The focus became stopping the behaviour and not trying to understand it. The support system that was built for him failed him. Poor understanding created a poorly built structure. Bad ideas led to bad results. I recollect a time where I had to rescue a dock-ramp counterweight that had fallen off. I had a plan, during low tide to retrieve it. I had my dad with me for this task and I told him of my idea. He replied, "Well that's *an* idea son…it's just not a good one." His years of being an ironworker and a millwright gave me a more efficient plan. Most of the ideas for supporting Brent were along those lines – ideas, yes, but not very good ones.

William Osler said, "The good physician treats the disease; the great physician treats the patient who has the disease." Brent's disease was his aggressive behaviour and it was only when he was seen as a person and not a behaviour did his life change for the better.

ONE THING CHECKED OFF THE BUCKET LIST

"Sometimes you will never know the value of a moment until it becomes a memory."

Unknown

Things improved for Brent. No longer fighting to be understood, it became easier to have him experience things that were previously unattainable to him. As noted a few times, Brent had favourite music and his musical tastes are similar to mine. The Rolling Stones, The Beatles, George Thorogood and Credence Clearwater Revival, to name a few. Brent, like me, gets some of the lyrics wrong. "Can't Buy Me Love," by The Beatles, comes out to Brent as, "Oh Bobby Love." There have been a few people who have come through Brent's life since leaving the Pink house. One such person is Mark. He has moved on but before he left he was responsible for a magical experience for Brent.

John Fogerty, the singer for CCR, was coming to town and Mark asked about taking Brent to go see him. I was not so sure it would be such a good idea, as Brent could be unpredictable. Mark was confident that he would be just fine and that he would accompany him. I relented, but I cautioned Mark to be prepared to leave at a moment's notice. I received a call from Mark and he told me that he made some inquiries and scored three tickets in the front row. Mark played the handicapped card and only had to pay for one ticket, since tickets for Brent's escorts were free. Mark also told them that Brent needed a wheelchair to get around. This was true as Brent is unsteady on his feet and he is a slow walker. This is how he obtained the front-row seats.

Mark was not exaggerating about the need for two support people for Brent…in the past. I was asked if I would be the second escort and I jumped at it. It was decided that we would forgo the first act and would wheel him in when John Fogerty got on stage. We took our position up front, the lights went down and I have since forgotten the first song but of course it was a CCR classic. What I do remember are the words Brent said, "He's here." Not sure what that meant. Did it mean that John Fogerty was here and he was seeing the face and the live voice of a song he had heard for years or that he, Brent, was here? It really does not matter what it meant. Brent was among thousands of other people, and fitting in. It was odd because months earlier the crisis team, and others, thought Brent was incapable of being around anybody without hitting them. All the time John Fogerty was belting out all those CCR hits, Brent was belting no one. Not sure if Brent has a bucket list but if he does, I would think attending that concert checked off a box.

IT'S NOT ALL ROSES

"I cannot do all the good that the world needs. But the world needs all the good I can do."

Jana Stanfield

In the pictures attached to this story, especially the most recent ones, it shows Brent smiling and by all accounts happy. Brent is not happy all the time. Things have changed for the positive for Brent. He isn't hitting staff. He does, at times of joy or playfulness, slap out at staff but only those he cares about. He telegraphs this with a wry smile and the warning, "You look here." He then lifts his arm high and slaps at you. He does not hit hard. His intent is not to hurt as it would have been in the past. It seems to be a way to draw some physical contact from someone he trusts. He will also ask for a hug, then slap your back or dig his fingers into your shoulder. This happens rarely, and is always done in fun.

The toughest thing for staff when supporting Brent is when he is in one of his frustration moods. He will become filled with internal demons, then the fight inside his head begins. These internal struggles can last for hours and although we try to help him through these times it takes its toll on the caregivers. We understand that he is probably reliving his early years at Woodlands and the self-abuse he inflicts is heartbreaking. You can take the person out of the institution but you can't take the memories out of the person. Things are mostly rosy for Brent with the exception of when his past comes back to haunt him.

CONCLUSION

"You can't go back and change the beginning, but you can start were you are and change the ending."

C.S. Lewis

Brent has come from being labelled many things: The Million Dollar Man, a monster, a staff-hurting machine and the second-most-difficult person in the entire province to support in the community. To now being described as loving, funny, mischievous and a charmer. A song written by Dewey Bunnell of the band America includes the lyrics: "Oz never gave nothing to the Tin Man that he didn't already have," I believe Brent had all those positive things inside him all along. My dad taught me to look for the goodness in people and that some had that goodness well hidden. It's the time taken to find that goodness that brings the benefits. Brent was, however, living in an environment that was controlling, punitive and unjust. When he was assaulted, he hit back; when freedoms were taken away he fought to get them returned and when he was dealt an injustice he would reply in kind. Nobody thought to pull back the curtain and look behind the aggression. What was he lacking in his life? What was this behaviour communicating? Those wishing to support him in the past were distracted by his behaviour and could not see past it. All it took to turn this around was to treat him with respect, to listen to not only his words but to his actions and to show him that you cared. Martin Luther King was quoted "Protest is the language of the unheard" Anger, aggression and violence was Brent's form of protest for not being heard. Brent does give as good as he gets; give him your respect and you will get his, show him love and you will be shown love from him. He does not need big men around him anymore to "keep him in line." He is now supported mostly by women who have only heard the stories of the past. No one working with him now has ever witnessed the rage he was so famous for.

Canadian philosopher Marshall McLuhan said, “Violence is a quest for identity. The less identity, the more violence.”

Brent was fighting for his identity and in this fight his violence became his identity, at least for those who could look no further than his aggression.

A person who is told or shown often enough that he is nothing, and is treated as a lesser human, he starts believing it himself. Brent was told this in words and actions towards him but he knew better. Bruce Cockburn wrote, “You have to kick at the darkness till it bleeds daylight.” Brent did just that: he refused to believe he was nothing. Once I and others saw that sliver of light, the same light that his mother saw, it was not hard to show others his brightness. As soon as others saw what I saw, it was Brent that took over the teaching. Nelson Mandela said, “When a man is denied the right to live the life he believes in, he has no choice to become an outlaw.” Brent wanted to be respected; he wanted to be loved and treated fairly. When this did not happen he became an outlaw.

I still have a copy of a profile of Brent written by the social worker who wanted him transferred back to Woodlands. In this profile he wrote many things that were misguided. The physical environment had to include unbreakable glass, walls of plywood and cameras - all things that were never implemented. The most interesting thing he said was, and this is a quote from that profile on what Brent needs: “He needs to learn how to love and to be loved.” This social worker had most of the words right. Brent didn’t need to learn how to love. He always knew how to love. What he needed was to teach us how to love him and over the past many years that is just what he has done.

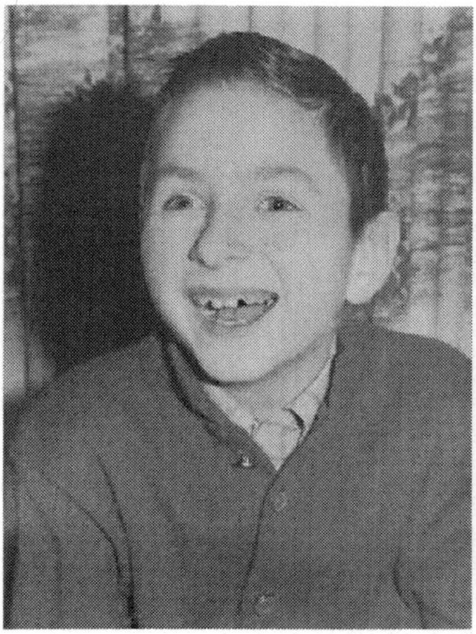

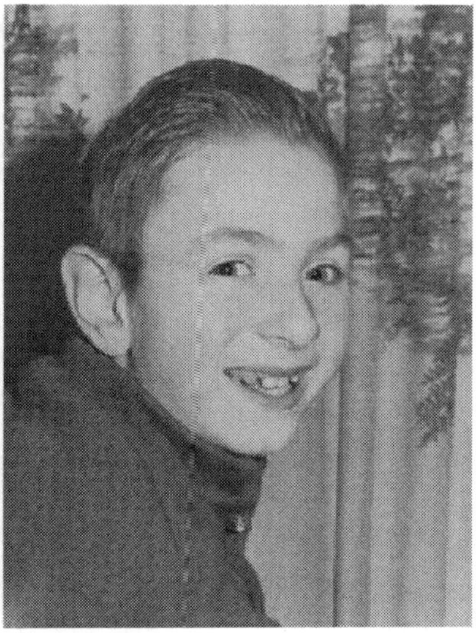

Brent at 8 years old just before being admitted to Woodlands.

Brent at 25 during a visit at his parents house.

Brent with his dad at 10 years old

Brent with his mom at 18 years old.

Brent had recently moved to the 'Pink House' and was out here on a whale watching tour. Seen here wearing his 'Hockey Turtleneck Sweater' as he liked to call it.

Brent happy with his new found freedoms to be able to choose what he wants to wear.
Seen here modelling his 'Jacket Raincoat'..

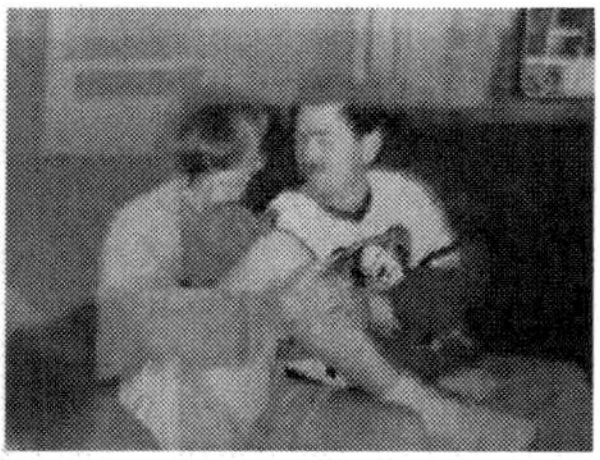

Brent's first of many visits to his sister Sherry's house wearing his new 'Hockey Turtle Neck Sweater' as his first one fell apart from too many washings. .

Brent with his housemate, Ian.

Brent on a 'Hydro Bus' ride. He calls all buses 'Hydro' because during his time at Woodlands some buses were powered by BC Hydro (electrical overhead) Lines.

Sheryl AKA Mamma with Brent having a 'sit down' coffee

Brent getting excited about one of his favourite meals: a cheeseburger.

A birthday celebration for Brent

Brent and Karen.
Seems he is not enraged with women with blonde hair, rather he's playful and loving with them.

Brent with his sister

Brent and Sheryl on a visit to "sister Sherry's" farm

Brent and Alysha.
This was when Alysha returned from maturnity leave. Brent missed her and he told her, "I love you to bits."

Notes and Sources:

1. Germany's assault on persons with disabilities, Burleigh, Michael. Death and Deliverance "Euthanasia" in Germany (1900-1945). Cambridge: Cambridge University Press, 1994.

2. Alfred Binet, Binet, A (1916) New Methods for the diagnoses of the intellectual level of sub normals.

3. Dr. Henry H. Goddard: Zenderland, L (1998) Measuring Minds: Henry Herbert Goddard and the origins of American intelligence Testing. New York University Press

4. Woodlands: de Courcy, Michael, A Long Last Look at Woodlands 1878 to 2003

5. "John Harvey Kellogg" Wikipedia http://en.wikipedia.org/wiki/John Harvey Kellogg

Acknowledgment and gratitude to the following:

Greig Cameron, he gave me my first push to write this story, and pushing me to publish.
Carol Matthews who after reading my first draft kindly offered invaluable advice and sent me on the path to turning this into a love story.
Marcus Hondro and Judith Phillips for their honesty. I believed that they both would have let me know if my zipper was down or I had spinach in my teeth, so with their encouragement I persisted.
I truly appreciate my friend and red penned editor Cam McCulloch who tolerated my constant miss-spelling, bad grammar and poor punctuation. He had way more patience for me than a drill that didn't work!
Steve Whittam for his graphic arts skills and many contributions to this book. Thanks Whits!
Jeffery Custeau for his photo of Brent and me on the back cover and for coming up with the title of the book.
Patti Odynski, who was the spoon that stirred the sauce when it came to my many run-ins with those in power.
Brent's Sister, Sherry Heisterman for her support in this endeavor. She is indeed a wonderful sister to Brent and a good friend to me.
Heaps of appreciation to my sister Linda and my Aunt Betty (Cousin Danny's mom) they have been my biggest cheerleaders, I love them to bits.
The staff of Namaste and Kjosa, thanks for being great learners and great humans and for caring for Brent the way they do.
Sincere love to my family, wife Julie, son Jake and daughter Marik for their patience and support while I worked the long days to keep Brent from ever setting foot in another institution. I am forever grateful to have you three in my life.

Finally, Brent, thanks for being the best teacher I have ever known.

Manufactured by Amazon.ca
Bolton, ON

16531641R00111